Ram Ram

Lord Zarathustra

Lord Buddha

Shankaracharya

Sri Ramana Maharishi

Sri Rama Krishna

Annie Besant

I HAVE COME NOT TO TEACH
BUT TO AWAKEN
"MEHER BABA"
AHMED NAGAR.

GREAT MYSTIC SAINTS OF THE WORLD

By

Yogi M.K. Spencer

Edited by

Prof. S.P. Ruhela
Sai Divine Research Centre
126, Sector 37 Faridabad 121 003

Regency Publications
New Delhi 110 008

First Published: 1947
Revised Edition: 1998
© S.P. Ruhela (1998)

No part of this book may be reproduced, except for reviews, without written permission from the publisher.

ISBN 81-86030-78-6

Published by Regency Publications, 20/36-G, Old Market, West Patel Nagar, New Delhi 110 008 and printed at Radiant Printers, New Delhi 110 008, Phones: 5712539, 574 0038 • Telefax: 578 3571.

DEDICATED

With all reverence and love
to
RISHI RAM RAM
the beloved Master of the spirit world
who has inspired me to write
this small volume
and
whose loving guidance from the
other world is like a beacon light
in the panorama of Life

GREETING GOD

God I greet Thee with eyes of love,
I see Thee shining from above
Thy smile is so radiant, Thy face so full of bliss;
Oh, let me bend down and Thy feet reverently kiss.

Thou art the fire of my soul, my heart's delight,
I live solely in Thy love and divine light.
My heart is linked with Thee like a golden chain;
I care not for any crumbs of earthly gain.

I leap with delight when I think of Thee.
It makes me radiant, joyous, free.
My heart's devotion is my soul's contentment.
I seek no other kind of lavishment.

Is it that I see the Masters clustering
From that deep beyond and shedding
Their lustrous light on this silent scene,
And make life's stream so sweet and serene?

Is it that I see the invisible with the inner eye,
All dipped in brightness with the deepest divine dye?
Is it God that I am seeing face to face?
It is all, oh Lord, Thy divine grace.

M.K. Spencer

EDITOR'S NOTE

Yogi Minocher K. Spencer (1888–1958) was an Indian Parsi who lived almost all his life in Karachi. He was deeply interested in divine mysteries. He served lepers in Karachi for thirty years. He was a medium and spiritual healer. He was a metal merchant in Karachi. This was his third and last birth. In His first birth in the 12th century in Italy he was Petricio, a Christian, who became a very inspired, dedicated and renowned preacher of Christianity and later founded the Order of Friars. His soul took second birth as a South Indian Hindu woman who became a house-wife and suffered much in her married life. However, she was an ever-willing and most altruistic and dedicated servant of her community, but she loved her children so much that her attachment to them came in her way to achieve liberation. The same soul took third birth in a Parsi family in Pune in India, and he got the name *Minnoo* or Minocher K. Spencer.

Right from the moment of his birth, Spencer was under the patronage and guidance of a great Spirit Master Rishi Ram Ram, appointed by God to spiritually train him to achieve liberation in this very birth. He got interested in Spiritualism when he visited a trance clairvoyant in London in 1937. Soon he became a medium. During 1941–1946, he seriously studied almost all the important scriptures and books of all religions and countless other spiritual books and materials.

On his divine Master's instructions, he went to meet the two great mystics of those times — Avatar Meher Baba and Maharshi Ramana in 1945 and 1947 respectively. He received their blessings and guidance to move on his path of spiritual uplife vigorously. His master Rishi Ram Ram used to appear regularly before him in his meditation and give him messages.

In his unique spiritual message of 11th may, 1949, Rishi Ram Ram told Spencer: "... you have passed all the stages for which I was competent to help you. You don't need the Master's help any more. God alone can now help you."

The same day, the Master put up the case of Spencer before Sai Baba and the latter said to him in his first direct spirit message: "Yes I am Sai Baba, come to you at the express desire of your beloved Master, Rishi Ram Ram, just to solve your difficulty."

At the time of the transfer of Spencer on 11th May, 1949, Rishi Ram Ram told Spencer, "I am handing you on to Him (Sai Baba) for He has the final authority to liberate your soul and not I." It was then revealed to Spencer by Rishi Ram Ram as well as Sai Baba (Shirdi Sai Baba) that Sai Baba was none other than God Himself in His '*Sakari*' (Manifest) aspect — the Highest in the Celestial Hierarchy. On 18th May, 1949, Rishi Ram Ram revealed the following secret to Spencer:

"I reveal to you this secret today. God is manifesting to you in the shape and form of Sai Baba. . . . He is Asho Ahura Mazda Amshaspand as well as God. You have heard Him. You will also soon see Him."

Sai Baba, the God Almighty trained Spencer spiritually in a very rigorous manner from 1949 to 1958. It was

Spencer's staunch wish and determination to find God — "see God face to face" — in his very birth, and ultimately God fulfilled this wish of this great yogi of modern India. A very thrilling account of his spiritual memoirs as such has been presented by Yogi Spencer in his book 'How I Found God', which was first published in 1958 in proof form only for a very limited circulation (only 100 copies had been printed as such) but as soon as the book was published God asked the author to burn all the book. This was God's test Whether there still existed any trace of ego in Yogi Spencer. Save with the exception of one or two copies all the copies of that 1396-page book were immediately put to flame.

After a gap of 40 years, by unique divine will I could get the only available copy of that rarest of the rare book. An abridged and edited version of that unique spiritual book of Yogi M.K. Spencer, prepared by me is soon going to be published, which, according to the divine messages of God, "will be hailed as new chapter in the history of man's progress — progress towards unification as opposed to separation" (Message on 7th March, 1957), ". . . will play a dominant part and your mission will be recognised as a forerunner of a great religious revolution not only in India but all over the world" (Message on 8th March, 1997), ". . . . The author of this book who has realised God in every sense of the word is appointed by God to fulfil God's mission of bringing light in darkness and raising man from the stagnation of life to the regions of eternal bliss. . ." (God's *Foreword* to the book.)

Sai Baba, the God almighty had assigned a unique mission to Yogi Spencer — to write rare book on spirituality for the enlightenment of the people of all religions and nations throughout the world. He wrote many beautiful books namely: *The Other World*,

Romance of A Soul, Oneness With God, Hymns, Joyous Mysticism, Light on the Path, Divine Discourses and Poems, Ramana Maharshi, Esoteric Poems of Devotion, Talks on Spiritual Philosophy and *Poems of the Heart.*

The author's original book *'Joyous Mysticism'* was in two parts. The material presented therein was related to two broad themes — Survey of Mysticism in World Religions, and profiles of world renowned mystics, viz Sri Rama Krishna, Sadhu Sunder Singh, Mahatma Gandhi, St. Francis of Assissi, Mystics of Medieval Europe (Meister Eckhart, St. Theresa, Ignatius Loyola, John Ruysbrook), Shankaracharya, George Fox, and Mrs. Annie Besant. As mentioned above, Spencer had personally met the great mystic Ramana Maharshi in July 1947 and was so much impressed with the great mystic of Arunachala that he wrote a separate small book on him (Ramana Maharshi).

I have reorganised and edited all these materials, and now brought out books — *'Joyous Mysticism in world Religions'* which presents an extensive and comprehensive survey of Mysticism, and the present book *'Great Mystic Saints of the World'*, which includes all the above mystics on which the divine-inspired Yogi Spencer had written with such spiritual ferver, lucidity and clarity.

I am deeply grateful to the three great divine Masters — Rishi Ram Ram, Sri Shirdi Sai Baba and Swami Amritanandaji (the present Spirit Guide of the World), the eminent author (Late) Yogi M.K. Spencer. Grateful thanks are offered to (Late) Sri K.S.D. Aiyer, Secretary, Spiritual Healing Centre, Coimbatore (now extinct), and my *'Spiritual Father'* and Sri A. Somasundaramji, Founder and Honorary Secretary of Divine Centre, Markapur (Andhra Pradesh). With the blessings of these Spirit Masters and these Spiritualists, I have been privileged to be associated with the editing and reproduction of these great works of Yogi Spencer on spirituality which will benefit eager seekers of Truth throughout the world.

18th June, 1998
Sai Divine Research Centre
126, Sector 37,
Faridabad 121003

SATYA PAL RUHELA
Professor of Education (Sociology)
Institute of Advanced Studies in Education
Jamia Millia Islamia
(Central University)
New Delhi-110 025

CONTENTS

INTRODUCTION

As we sit in a secluded corner and behold nature, the thought that arises in our mind is, "There is nothing in this world, but life." The whole universe from the atom to the sky is pulsating with life. And this life is one, though the forms are many. God is one though He manifests Himself in diverse ways. He is the only Reality. The mystic knows this truth by actual experience. There is within him an awareness of God — God who is both transcendental and immanent in nature. It is all radiant light that he sees. His vision takes him to the starry avenue. He climbs the starry ladder step by step till he reaches the abode of the Cosmic Spirit — God.

Mystics have existed for ages past. They have marched through the corridor of time. Their mysticism has helped this world to go forward in endless ways.

Life is like an endless stream ever flowing from the Unmanifest and going back to the ocean of its origin — God. The mystics understand the secrets of nature. Christ said, "I will utter things which have been kept secret from the foundation of the world." (St. Matthew 13:35). But it is a question whether Christ was really the first to give a new message. What He taught and what demonstrations He gave of His yogic and super-normal powers were no new revelations at all. The yogis and mystics of the ages long before Christ had known the secrets of nature.

Readers will kindly pardon me for making some personal references in regard to the writing of this book. A message was got from Coimbatore, in 1946, that Rishi Ram Ram had selected two of the members of the Spiritual Healing Centre to write books on behalf of the Centre. One of the two selected was myself. I therefore, invoked Rishi Ram Ram on 15th September, 1946, to suggest a title for the book and He gave the following long title: "Joyous Mysticism to lighten mankind into the worship of God" and I was further told: "Write when I inspire you."

This humble work is the result of patient labour. It will be evident that it has not the mark of scholarship, though I was fortunately, in a position to read and study a good number of books, chiefly from the libraries of the local Theosophical Society and the Spiritual Healing Centre, Coimbatore. A fair study of the subject was necessary before Rishi Ram Ram could undertake to inspire me. This book is entirely the result of the Master's inspiration — only the blemishes are mine.

I express my gratitude to my friend in Bombay, who refuses to allow me to disclose his name, for reading the manuscript as usual and for making his observations. I am also grateful to Mr. Phillipowsky, a member of the editorial staff of *The Daily Gazette*, Karachi, for making certain corrections. I am greatly indebted to my dear friend, Mr. Doraswami Iyer, the indefatigable secretary of the Spiritual Healing Centre, Coimbatore, for undertaking to get the book published on behalf of the Centre.

M.K. Spencer

Karachi
24th June, 1947

1

ST. FRANCIS OF ASSISSI

There have been instances of sick souls becoming saints and mystics. Count Leo Tolstoy was a sick soul. He drank deep of the cup of the pleasures of life. He had money to squander about. But all his wealth and position did not give him an iota of happiness. In fact, he became ultimately so disgusted with his life that he was on the verge of committing suicide. In his book, *My Confession,* we get an account of his melancholy life. We see him battling and struggling. We see him losing all appetite for life's values. We see him groping for something on which he could rest his soul, as an escape from life's delusions. His aching heart is crying for relief. He is enveloped in a strange feeling of dread, which gnaws his heart, though outwardly he appears as fortune's favoured child. But, gradually, there comes in him the craving for God. It completely changes his attitude towards life. The feeling of dread and loneliness gradually gives place to that of joy and hopefulness. He gives up all pleasures of the senses and takes to a life of simplicity and austerity. He lives by faith. "Faith is the sense of life, that sense by virtue of which man does not destroy himself but continues to live on. It is the force whereby we live. If man were not to believe that he must live for something, he would not live at all. The idea of an infinite God, of the divinity of the soul, of the union of man's actions with God — these are ideas elaborated in the infinite depths of the human thought. They are ideas without which there would be no life, without which I myself," said Tolstoy, "would not exist. I began to see that I had no right to rely on any individual reasoning and neglect those answers given by faith for they are the only answers to the question."

As soon as Tolstoy discovered the value of faith in divinity, his life changed. He began to say, "Believe in the infinite as common people do and life grows possible again."

Let us get into the inside of Tolstoy's mind to understand the cause of the great change in his life. He says, "I remember one day in early spring. I was alone in the forest lending my ear to its mysterious noises. I listened and my thought went back to what for these three years it always was busy with — the quest of God. But the idea of Him, I said, how did I ever come by the idea?"

"And again there arose in me with this thought, glad aspirations towards life. Everything in me awoke and received a meaning. Why do I look further? — a voice within me asked. He is there: He without whom one can not live. To acknowledge God and to live are one and the same thing.

God is what life is. Well then, live, seek God and there will be no life without Him."

Such was the transformation in Tolstoy. It is the same transformation that we meet when we recount the life-story of St. Francis of Assisi, one of the finest types of mystic saints in medieval Europe. He was born in 1182 at Assisi, a small town in Italy. His father was a trader and the boy as he grew up showed no inclination to study in any school and played away his time. He was fond of street amusements and led a care-free, merry life, holding everything that was holy and religious in condemnation.

But at the age of 25 a great change came over him. He fell seriously ill. The illness transformed him. What he once held in contempt, he began to revere and admire. He was imbued with a strange feeling for religion. His soul cried for God. He made poverty his bride and joined a troop of mendicant beggars, roaming from place to place. He would seek out lepers, kiss them, fondle them and show to them his utmost love and compassion. His father was annoyed at this strange behaviour of his son.

One day, as Francis was meditating near the ruins of the old church of St. Damien he heard a voice whisper to him: "Francis seest thou not that my house is in ruins; go and restore it for me."

To Francis it was a command. He had no money of his own. He lifted a bale from his father's shop, put it on the horseback, went to the market and sold it off along with the horse. The money, he realized from the sale, he handed over to the priest in charge of the ruined chapel, for its rebuilding and repairs, to the utter amazement of all concerned. When the news of his having stolen the property reached the ears of his father, he became red with rage. It was too preposterous that his son should have stolen his property. The motive behind the action was not understood. He considered it as an heinous crime and threatened to take deterrent action against his son.

Francis soon left his parental house in search of God. He was penniless but he did not feel of the least pinch. He remembered the teaching of the Bible: "Provide neither gold nor silver nor brass in your purses nor scrips for your journey, neither two coats, nor yet staves." He remembered also, "Sell all that thou hast and give to the poor then thou shall have treasure in heaven."

Having taken the vow of poverty and utter renunciation he went about preaching Christ's gospel to all the people. Fired by a religious enthusiasm which knew no bounds, he at once started organising forces for the formation of a society of religious brotherhood. He founded the Order of the Mendicants in the year 1208, with just seven disciples who gathered round his standard. He was not deterred by the thinness of the number of his disciples. Such was the fire and determination in him coupled with faith in God that he met with success as he went onward in his spiritual adventure and the order founded by him is today a formidable organisation of the church, playing an important role in life.

The following words which Francis spoke to his first disciples, are replete with so much of warmth of feeling and prophecy that it is worth reproducing the whole address:

"Fear not because you are small and seem foolish. Have confidence in the Lord, who has vanquished the world. Some will revere you. Many proud will resist you. Bear all with sweetness and patience. Soon the wise and the noble will be with us. The Lord hath given me to see this. I have in my ears the sounds of the languages of all the people who will come to us, — French, Spanish, Germans, English. The Lord will make us a great people even to the end of this earth."

What prophetic words? The small and seemingly foolish people became the founders of an institution which today claims a world wide recognition.

When he sent his disciples on the mission of human service, he addressed them as under: "Go and preach two and two. Preach peace and patience; tend the wounded, relieve the distressed; reclaim the erring; bless those who persecute you and pray for them that despitefully use you."

The papal sanction was given to the formation of the Order, though there was some hesitancy in the beginning.

St. Francis founded also an Order of Poor Sisters on the same model as of Franciscan Brothers. Such were the feelings excited among the people, that they flocked to him asking for admission in a larger and larger numbers. St. Francis was a man of judgment. He did not like that the institution should suffer by admission of those whose worldliness was a formidable obstacle. For such of them, he founded an order called the Brethren of Penitence. They were not asked to take the vows of poverty and renunciation. They were asked to live in their own homes with their families but were admonished to abstain from pleasures, such as of going to theatres and dances. Evelyn Underhill pays the following tribute to St. Francis of Assissi in her book, "*Mysticism.*"

"The fact that St. Francis wrote little and lived much, that his actions were of unequalled simplicity and directness, long blinded his admirers to the fact that he is a typical mystic: the only one perhaps who forced the most trivial and sordid circumstances of sensual life to become perfect expressions of Reality."

One can get an idea of his renunciation from the fact that like Indian *sanyasins*, St. Francis made it a point to eat the remnants of food which the public gave to him, without any shudder. A further idea of his exalted spirit, we get from the fact, that though his artistic mind at first revolted at the loathesome sight of a leper, he got over that feeling and did not mind even embracing and kissing the unfortunate person. Such was his great will and love of God and men that he would tame his artistic soul to look upon even the most sordid and repulsive side of nature as God's bounty. He looked upon the lice in his undergarment as "celestial pearls."

St. Francis was a perfect type of *Karma Yogi* and a *Bhakta.* He worked and served without the least expectation of any return or reward. The following lines are significant of the dedicated life which St. Francis himself led.

> "Blessed is he that truly loves and seeketh not love in return.
>
> "Blessed is he that serves and desires not to be served in return.
>
> "Blessed is he that doeth good unto others and seeketh not that others do good to him."

What idealism? St. Francis practised every word, he preached. He was a great lover of all kinds of animals and birds. He saw and understood the mystic unity of all in the universe. Birds and animals were as much his friends, brothers and messengers of God, as men themselves. His gentility, his humanity, his poetic and artistic nature, coupled with a warm heart that responded to the crises of all who suffered, make St. Francis of Assisi one of the most laudable figures in the galaxy of medieval catholic saints.

2

ADI SHANKARACHARYA

India has produced two intellectual and spiritual giants of the highest order viz., the great Buddha, whose religion is followed to-day by nearly one-third of the whole human race and Shankaracharya, the ablest exponent of the *Advaita philosophy, Yogin of Yogins,* whose skill dialectic philosophy, none has so far been able to surpass. Shankaracharya is considered to be a man of unusual intellectual capacity. He was an intellectual prodigy. Marvellous stories are related of his wonderful precocity. It is said that in the very first year of his life, he picked up the whole of the Sanskrit alphabet. At the age of two he learned to read; at the age of three he understood by intuition several portions of the Scriptures. At the age of seven he had studied and mastered the *Puranas,* the *Mahabharata,* the *Smrtis* and the *Shastras.*

We do not know exactly where and in what year he was born. There are conflicting reports about the place and date of his birth. A lot of legendary stories has been woven round the thread of his life. Some believe that he flourished in the second century after Christ. Others think that he lived ten centuries after Christ. We have no authentic account of the life and doings of the great philosopher and mystic. His commentaries of the *Upanishads,* the *Bhagvad Gita* and other Scriptural writings and the information that we get from *Shankaravijayas or Triumphs of Shankara* reveal him to us as a man of extraordinary intellectual and spiritual powers. It is no wonder that Madame Blavatsky refers to his extraordinary occult and yogic powers in her work, *The Secret Doctrine.* The following lines from the pen of Mrs. Annie Besant should give us an idea of the supra-intellectual and spiritual man, that Shankaracharya undoubtedly was: "From the occult standpoint the first Shri Shankaracharya was a Being far above our race, one of the Three Kumaras, immediately below the Great Initiator, spoken of in *The Secret Doctrine* and in closest relation with Him. He belongs to the humanity of Shukra, not to that of our earth. He became incarnate about eighty years after the passing away of Gautama, the Lord Buddha — a fact which is historically recorded only in the archives of the Dwarka Matt. Some hints about him may be found in the third volume of *The Secret Doctrine,* but they are very confused and perhaps purposely made contradictory; they will be found in the section on *The Mystery of Buddha.*"

It is said at the age of eight, Shankara donned the yellow robe. His mother was strongly against his becoming a *sanyasin,* as she was deeply attached to him, more so, as he had once saved her life, by his inherent occult powers. Madhav, his biographer relates the following incident, ending in Shankara's gaining permission from his reluctant mother to join the brotherhood of *sanyasins.* One day, while bathing in the river, his foot was caught by an alligator. He called loudly and his loud moaning reached the ears of his mother. She rushed to her son, who implored her to save his life, which she could do only if she gave him permission to become a *sanyasin.* Coerced in this manner, she gave her permission reluctantly. Shankaracharya then jumped out of the water, the alligator having let go its hold on his leg.

The boy then wandered from place to place, going through jungles and forests, climbing hills and crossing rivers and unconscious of his surroundings. His mind and heart were all fixed on God. A boy of mere eight years of age, of precocious intellect and unsurpassed energy, flies from the world in search of Eternity. He makes his hermitage by the side of a cave near the banks of the Nerbudda and he is initiated by his guru Govind Yati who teaches him the secrets of the Sacred Science. He realizes the deep significance of the *Mahavakyas* in the *Vedas,* which speak of man's identification with Brahman, the Eternal, the Infinite, the Supreme, the Absolute. *So'ham* I am He, *Aham Brahmasmi,* I am Brahman, *Tattvamasi,* Thou art That, *Atma Brahman,* This soul is Brahman, *Gnan Brahmam,* Knowledge is Brahmam.

It is said that when his guru was in *samadhi,* this young lad after he had been initiated in the mysteries of the *Vedas,* pronounced certain mystic verses and he was able to do the miracle of quelling the tempest of rain. When his guru returned from his *samadhi,* he was overjoyed to witness the miracle performed by his pupil and he was convinced in his mind regarding the extraordinary intellectual and spiritual powers of the young lad. He gave him his blessings and asked him to go to Benares and enter upon his glorious work of saving mankind.

Shankara goes to Benares and soon becomes a famous *yogi.* People flock to him to become his pupils. At the tender age of twelve, we are told, he takes men as his chelas of whom Padmapada becomes the most favourite.

Sankaracharya soon distinguishes himself in dialectics and philosophy. He engages himself in writing his famous commentaries on the *Brahma Sutras,* the *Upanishads* and the *Bhagvad Gita.* His deep learning and scholarship, his oratorical talents, his skill in debate and his yogic powers create many adversaries, who come from distant places to challenge his superiority of knowledge. We are told that even Vyasa, the reputed author of the *Vedanta Sutras,* an old man, came to see the young lad, at his hermitage and entered into a disputation with him on certain knotty points in the Vedantic philosophy and was quite surprised and convinced of the natural gift of the young lad who seemed to have learnt by intuition rather than by deep study of the Scriptures, the entire philosophy of the *Vedas*.

Shankaracharya undertook to travel from place to place through out India on the mission of spreading the knowledge of the Vedas. The royal princes and chiefs offered him assistance in every way. His was a triumphant march. He dislodged all critics and adversaries by means of his impenetrable logic and argument and clearness of thought. His was the real missionary spirit and he succeeded in his mission. He raised eloquent war against the Buddhistic decadence that had set in. He brought out many reforms. He fought against animal sacrifices. He exposed the hypocrisy of the monks and nuns. He worked like a Trojan to revive Hinduism in its prestine glory. He laid firmly in the hearts of his followers the seed of the essence of true Vedantic teaching viz. of the One God, the Absolute Spirit, the One without a second in place of multiple gods and goddesses that the people worshipped.

The anecdote regarding his controversy with Mandana Mishra, a great and learned Pandit, who lived in affluent style is related in several biographies of Shankaracharya, which shows the importance of the event. Mandana who was married to a most accomplished and learned woman by the name of Bharati, challenged Shankaracharya, who was an exponent of the Vedantic philosophy and an upholder of religious celibacy. Mandana who was brought up in *Karma Mimamsa* faith, considered *sanyasins* as wasters, hypocrites and parasites. He was opposed to the monastic system.

Shankaracharya accepted the challenge of Mandana. When he came to his palace, the gates were closed. He therefore by his yogic powers inspite of the doors being closed entered into the very room where Mandana was seated. The latter got excited by the entry of the Yogi in this sudden and miraculous manner. They immediately entered into hot discussion, each vindicating the merits of his case. Bharati was made the umpire. She put two garlands, one on the neck of her husband and the other on the neck of Shankaracharya, the great yogi and she said: "He who is defeated in his argument will find the flowers of the garland fade away."

In the hot discussion that soon ensued Mandana was defeated. His garland faded away. He felt crest-fallen but as promised he agreed to put on the yellow robe and become a meek follower of Shankaracharya. But his wife who was too shrewd raised the point, that Shankara by defeating Mandana had not won, for she being the wife of her husband she must also be allowed to enter into the controversy and Shankara must defeat her before he can claim his victory.

Shankara accepted the challenge. Bharati knew well that the *sanyasi* would not be able to reply to her, if she raised a question regarding the Science of Love, unknown to *sanyasins*. It was too true. Shankaracharya was for a moment baffled. He asked leave to present himself after a month. The leave was granted.

Shankaracharya was a Raja Yogi. He knew how to separate his soul from his body. He saw the corpse of a king by name Amaruka being carried to the burning ghat for cremation. He informed his disciples of his plan to transfer his soul to the dead body of the king and asked them to take care of his body till his soul returned to occupy it. Those who came to the funeral of the king were astonished to see the body become alive. They carried their king again to the palace.

Shankaracharya then led a gay life in the body of the deceased king. He got the experience that he wanted. After some time he went back to the place where his empty body was lying and transfered his soul to it. Thus Shankaracharya was again in his original body and quite fit to enter into the battle of wits with Bharati, the wife of Mandana. He soon defeated her, having gained experience in a novel way and she admitted her defeat. The husband and the wife then both took the vows of renunciation and entered the monastic order.

There will be many who may disbelieve the veracity of the above anecdote. But students of *yoga* know that it is possible to perform the feat of transferring one's soul from one's body to any other place. Patanjali includes it in the list of *siddhis*, which a *raja yogi* can perform.

Shankara had given a promise to his mother that when she died he would perform her funeral ceremonies. Though he was far away from his mother's place he got prophetic knowledge of her declining health and immediately repaired to her house, leaving all his disciples. When he met her, he consoled her with what little of his philosophy she could understand and she died peacefully. According to the prevalent custom, no *sanyasi* could attend to any funeral ceremony and his friends and relations strongly objected to his presence. But he refused to budge an inch. All deserted him and he was left alone with the dead body. He produced fire from his hand and cremated his mother's body.

What a powerful memory Shankaracharya had, we can realize from the fact that when his favourite pupil Padmapada, returning from a pilgrimage told him that his commentary on the *Bhashya*, which he had kept with his uncle, had been destroyed by him, he dictated the whole of it to Padmapada from memory.

He travelled very extensively through out the country, from north to south and east to west. While travelling in Assam an attempt was made on his life by a man named Pandit Abhinava Gupta, who had sustained defeat at his hands in a philosophic debate. Being an adept in Black Magic, he caused Shankaracharya to suffer from an incurable disease. Doctors were consulted but they could not do any thing. His life was given up. Shankara bore his malady patiently but his disciples were considerably upset. It is said that the Black Magician's plot was soon found out and Padmapada, himself also a magician counteracted the evil effect and Shankara was saved. But he did not live long. The effects of the disease had shaken his constitution and he expired at Kedernath, some say in his thirty-second and some in his thirty-eighth year. Thus passed away one of the most dynamic personalities in the East — nay of the world.

It is not our purpose to enter into detailed survey of his teaching. But a few broad lines of his philosophy are necessary in order to understand the sublimity of the soul of this great sage and mystic. He was the greatest exponent of the *Advaita* philosophy and lover of *Bhagvad Gita,* which may be considered as the greatest book in mysticism.

The first principal teaching is, that Brahman alone is Real and all else is *maya, avidya,* ignorance, delusion, illusion. It is *maya* or ignorance that acts like a smoke screen and hides the Reality. It is this screen that we must remove to see the Reality, which alone counts and which alone is Eternal.

The soul is the immortal spark of the Absolute Spirit, which is Brahman. In order to realize self, the sheets which cover the soul must be removed one by one. We must transcend the barriers created by these sheets. These sheets are variously named:

(1) *Annamaya Kosha,* the nutritive or material sheet, (2) *Pranamaya Kosha,* the vital sheet, (3) *Manomaya Kosha,* the intellectual sheet, (4) *Vignanmaya Kosha,* the discriminating or analysing sheet and (5) *Anandamaya Kosha* the beatific sheet.

These *koshas* or sheets or coats, hide the real nature of the self, just as a scabbard encloses a sword and keeps it hidden from view. The soul in its lowest stage identifies itself with the physical body. Pleasures form the worst type of "maya." The Gita speaks of these maya-mad people in the following verses:

> "Filled with insatiable desires, full of hypocrisy, pride and arrogance holding unwholesome views through delusion, they work with unholy resolve;
>
> "Beset with immense cares ending only with death, sensual enjoyment their highest aim, assured that that is all;
>
> "Bound by hundreds of bands of hope, given over to lust and wrath, they strive to secure by unjust means hoards of wealth for sensual enjoyments.
>
> "This to-day has been gained by me; this desire I shall attain; this is mine and this wealth shall also be mine in future.
>
> "That enemy has been slain by me and others also shall I slay. I am a lord, I enjoy. I am successful, strong and healthy.
>
> "I am rich and well-born. Who else is equal to me? I will sacrifice, I will give,

> I will rejoice." Thus deluded by unwisdom.
>
> "Bewildered by many a fancy, entangled in the snare of delusion, addicted to the gratification of lust, they fall into a foul hell."
>
> (Discourse XVI, 10–16)

The soul for its purification must give up the gross matter of the body and in the above lines of the Gita we have a graphic picture of what it is. The next stages in spiritual evolution are the control of our emotions and our mind, both the lower and the higher. And when we come to the stage, when the subject and the object are reflected as one, we then get the true light of Reality. We are in bondage when we identify ourselves with limited objects, which cause sin and misery. The moment we get the consciousness of unity with the Supreme Spirit, we get our liberation, the end and object of life.

What is the method of gaining this liberation? The *Bhagvad Gita* lays down the three paths that lead to union with God. These are (1) *The Karma Marga,* (2) *The Jnana Marga* and (3) *The Bhakti Marga.* These three paths of action, wisdom and devotion have the same goal and eventually blend into one, acquiring the qualities of all the three paths. Speaking of *Karma Yoga,* the Gita says:

"None, verily, even for an instant ever remains doing no action; for everyone is driven helpless to action by energies born of nature.

"He who, restraining the organs of action, sits thinking in his mind of the objects of the senses, self-deluded, he is said to be one of false conduct.

"But who so restraining the senses by mind, O, Arjuna, engages in *Karma Yoga,* unattached with organs of action, he is esteemed.

"Do thou perform thy bounden duty: for action is superior to inaction. And even the maintenance of the body would not be possible for thee by inaction.

"Except in the case of action for sacrifice's sake, the world is action bound. Action for the sake thereof, do thou, O son of Kunti, perform, free of attachment."

(Discourse III, 5–9)

Absence of all motion is the worst sin. To do nothing, to be actuated by no impulse or desire is the stage of darkness, sloth, *tamash,* which is the worst evil in life. Even an active, wicked man, with wicked designs is better than an indolent, lazy parasitic, who lives on the dole of others and does absolutely no work for love or money.

The propellers of action are desires good or bad. Unworthy desires debase man and shut him out from the door of spirituality. Good desires kindle consciousness in man for the progress of the world. But to work without expectation of any return or reward, without any kind of attachment to the objects of the senses is the *Karma Yogi's* religion. To work in the expectation of gaining heaven after death is also not allowed in the path of yoga. Perfect renunciation of fruit of labour, to do duty for the sake of duty and no other end, is the teaching of *Karma Yoga*. It is also necessary to maintain a balanced mind in all vicissitudes of life, in success or failure, pleasure or pain, honour or dishonour. How beautifully is it said in the Gita:

> "When thy mind perplexed by what thou hast heard, shall stand firm and steady in the Self, then wilt thou attain yoga."
>
> (Discourse II, 53)

When the *Yogin* asks for nothing, seeks nothing, refuses nothing, is not affected by anything in life and simply works and does his duty, whatever it be, living in a hovel or a palace, he is on the sure path of perfection. The heart purified of all desires gets then the glimpse of the Supreme.

> "Steadfast in devotion do thy work, O Dhananjaya, casting off attachment,

> being the same in success or failure. Evenness is called *Yoga*."
>
> (Bhagvad Gita, Discourse II, 48)

> "That man attains peace, who abandoning all desires moves about without attachment, without selfishness, without vanity."
>
> (Bhagvad Gita, Discourse II, 71)

The second path is that of *Gnan* i.e. wisdom. It is fraught with difficulties and it is only the few that can tread it, unlike the other two paths which are open to all. The prerequisites for this path are a lofty intellect, dispassionate discretion, the ability to see God in every bit of the universe, the desire to treat everyone as part and parcel of God, to consider the sinner and the saint with equal eyes, endurance and persistence to reach the goal at any cost. The course of the *Karma Yogi* is from attachment to non-attachment. The *Gnan Yogi* begins with knowledge based on observation and classification of external phenomena and objects and ends with wisdom, which is discrimination to discover Self in every part of the universe. The *gnan yogi* must have full control over his mind and body and full confidence in his own divinity. When the *gnan yogi* begins to discriminate the real from the unreal, the substance from the shadow, the eternal from the transient, he gets disgusted with the *maya* of the world and seeks solitude and silence, the unassailable instruments in seeking God. He sees the One in the multitudinous forms of the Many. His joy is transcendental. His gaze is fixed on the centre of the circle and not its circumference. The Gita describes *gnan yoga* in the following verses:

> "Absence of attachment for objects of the senses and also absence of egoism; perception of evil in birth, death and old ·age, in sickness and pain;
>
> "Unattachment, absence of affection for son, home and the like and constant equanimity in the attainment of the desirable and the undesirable;
>
> "Unflinching devotion to Me in Yoga of non-separation, resort to solitary places, distaste for the society of men;
>
> "Constancy in Self-knowledge, perception of the end of the knowledge of truth. This is declared to be knowledge and what is opposed to it is ignorance."
>
> (*Bhagvad Gita* Discourse XIII, 8–11)

The *Bakti Marga*, of all the paths is the easiest to tread and it is open to all. We have shown that the object of the gnan yogi is to strive for union with the Unmanifested, the Absolute, the all pervading Spirit, without form, Eternal and Infinite. The object of the *Bhakta* is Ishvera, the Manifest God. The work of the devotee becomes easy, when the object of devotion is a concretised form.

The *Bhakta* is a person with intense longing for God. This intense longing comes by constant practice of meditation and prayers. The Gita speaks of the Supreme Being in the following very beautiful verses:

> "The Supreme Brahman, the Supreme Light, the Supreme Purifier Thou art. All the *Rishis* declare Thee as Eternal, Divine Purusha, the Primal God, Unborn, Omnipotent, so said the divine sage Narada, as also Asita, Devala and Vyasa and Thou Thyself always sayest so to me."
>
> (Discourse X, 12, 13)

> "Thou thyself knowest Thyself as the Self, O Purusha Supreme, O Source of all beings, O Lord of beings, O God of Gods, O Ruler of the world."
>
> (Discourse X, 15)

> "Thou art the Imperishable, the Supreme Being, worthy to be known. Thou art the great Abode of the universe. Thou art the undying Guardian of the Eternal Dharma, Thou art the Ancient Purusha, I deem."
>
> (Discourse XI, 18)

Shankaracharya spoke of two kinds of vision, — that of the eye which was transient and fleeting and that of the self, which was eternal and lasting. He likewise spoke of two kinds of hearing, that of the ear, which was transient and of the self which was eternal. He spoke of knowledge and ignorance. In fact, his chief teaching revolves round the substance of the Reality, which is Eternal. It is more our ignorance, that attaches value to the world of time and space, which truly speaking has no existence. It is only by the light of the real knowledge of the Reality,said Shankaracharya that the veil of ignorance which leads men into darkness and sorrow can be lifted and the heart filled with Divine consciousness, leading to joyousness. *Avidya, Maya* — it is bondage. Knowledge, Light, Wisdom — it is liberation.

In fact, when the heart is purified, there is no necessity for religious ceremonies, no need for domestic duties. The man is then fit to worship God and God alone. There is no further necessity for him to stay in the household and do household duties. He could retire from the world, do such actions as may strengthen his bonds of love with God and increase his inward illumination.

The following concluding lines of the Bhagvad Gita apply beautifully to the life and character of Sri Shankaracharya, one of the greatest mystics, the world has produced:

"Resorting to a sequestered spot, eating but little, speech and body and mind subdued, always engaged in meditation and concentration, endued with dispassion:

"Having abandoned egotism, strength, arrogance, desire, enmity, property, free from the notion of "mine" and peaceful, he is fit to become Brahman.

"Becoming Brahman, of serene self, he neither grieves nor desires, treating all beings alike: he attains supreme devotion to Me.

"By devotion he knows Me in truth, he forthwith enters into Me."

(Discourse XVIII, 52–55.)

3

GERMAN MYSTICS OF MEDIEVAL EUROPE

When we look upon the lives of mystic Saints of medieval Europe, what we feel is whether self-mortification — in some instances taken to the extreme limit of bodily torture of repellant nature — is justifiable. Take, for example, the case of that great German mystic saint Heinrich Suso of Constance (1295–1366). He was a man of poetical fancy. He led a life of rigid austerity and his autobiography relates to us of the terrible mortification that he subjected himself to. He used to put on an under-garment striped with leather in which were fixed sharp pointed nails, turned towards the flesh. Every night he put it on, when he returned from hard work and we can imagine the terrible agony of his body, especially when he had to sleep on a bed covered with noxious insects. Practically the flesh was pierced and the blood would ooze out from the torn flesh. What an iron-will he must have possessed to have gone through such a terrible ordeal. And he did it for years together, dressing the wounds and again putting on the nailed garment to re-tear the flesh.

Suso used to live in a cell not more than four and half feet in length and mostly slept sitting or resting in the cell. His sleeping hours were not more than an hour and a half or two at most.

There are very few among European mystics who endured bodily mortification to the extent of Henry Suso. It is said that he practised it for full sixteen years and then he heard the voice of God, asking him to leave it off. It was said that such was the artistic genius of Suso, that had he not taken to mysticism, he would have shone as a great artist and poet. A great scholar —his auto-biography is a standard book on religious experiences—Suso's life is full of romantic beauty. He got visions. They "floated up as if it were from the subliminal region without disturbing thee course of his conscious life."

Suso enjoyed ecstasies and raptures in their fullest form. His soul was as if it were rapt in his body. The ecstasies were followed by great physical pains but he did not mind them. In fact, he said: "If that which I see and feel be not the kingdom of heaven, I know not what it can be: for it is very sure that the endurance of all possible pains were but a poor price to pay for the eternal possession of so great a joy."

It is said about St. Louis of Gonzaga, another mystic of Europe, that he carried his notion of purity of mind to such an extent, even at the age of twelve, if his mother who was of noble family and lived in a palatial house, sent her maid of honour by chance to convey to him any message, he would not allow her to come in his presence. He joined the Jesuit Order at the age of seventeen and died very young. He cultivated silence and remained by himself all day long, reading books and devoting his attention all the time to God. He avoided seeing the face of any woman. He never touched a flower, lest he may inhale its fragrance. If he at all talked or discussed, it was only on the subject of religion. All other subjects were absolute taboo to him. When his father dies, he wrote a letter to his mother arrogating to himself spiritual superiority and saying that his father's death was God's particular attention shown to him. Rightly has Rama Krishna said: "The vanities of others may die out but the vanity of a saint as regards his sainthood is hard indeed to wear out."

Poverty has been idealized in ancient Scriptures but no where is the mortification of the flesh and such rigid austerity commended. In fact, the *Bhagvad Gita* teaches that worldly actions have to be renounced by those who are still inwardly attached to them. But for a man of equanimity of mind, for one who has gained complete control over himself no austerities are necessary. Mortification of the flesh used to be practised in ancient India on a large scale by all those who took to the life of the forest in search of God. It was however, Buddha who taught the middle course. God, who is the Ocean of Bliss wants us all to be full of joy like Him. He can not be happy if we mortify our flesh, for our body is after all the temple of our soul and the perfection of bodily movement is a *sine-qua-non* in leading a truly religious and yogic life.

William James in his beautiful book, *The Varieties of Religious Experiences — a Study in Human Nature,* says, "Modern opinion has changed and we no longer hold corporeal mortification in respect. A Suso or a St. Peter appear to us to-day in the light of tragic mounte banks rather than sane men, inspiring us with respect. If the inner dispositions are right what need of all the mortification?"

Meister Eckhart

There is very little known of the life of that great German mystic, Meister Eckhart, who was born about the year 1260 and who died in 1327 or 1329; accounts vary. He was reputed for learning and was a distinguished son of the Church. He was a professor in one of the colleges in Paris. Though an Aristotalian in his philosophic beliefs his works teem with the ideas and inspiration gathered from the mystical writings of neo-Platonists. He is considered to be one of the first speculative mystics. The distinguished trait of his mysticism is that he unites reason with emotion. His mysticism is therefore not only emotional but is based also on speculative thought. He distinguished between Godhead and God. According to him the Godhead is the Absolute Essence which can never be described or be known by man nor is it even knowable to itself. Its chief characteristic is its *indeterminateness.* But in this Godhead lies the potentiality of the entire creation, which is not only its temporal act but "an eternal necessity." In order to understand Eckhait's mysticism, it is better to put it as far as possible in his own subtle language. He says; "I am as necessary to God as God is necessary to me. In my knowledge and love God knows and loves Himself. The eye with which I see God is the same eye with which God sees me. My eye and God's eye, are one eye, one vision, one recognition, one love."

The above teaching of Eckhart harmonises with the mystic teaching of that great Persian Sufi poet, Jalalud' Din Rumi, who says:

> "No lover ever seeks union with his
> beloved But his beloved is also seeking
> union with him.
>
> But the lover's love makes his body lean
>
> While the beloved's love makes her fair
> and lusty.
>
> When in this heart the lightning spark
> of love arises,
>
> Be sure this love is reciprocated in that
> heart,
>
> Without doubt God also feels love for
> thee.

It is a love chase. It is the fusion of the human with the divine nature.

"I am a Lamp to thee who beholdest Me,
I am a mirror to thee who perceivest Me,
I am a door to thee, who knockest Me,
I am a way to thee, a wayfarer."

God is near to us. He is in every stone and shrub, only that the stone and shrub are not aware of His Spirit. We are also not aware that God is standing at the very door of our heart and that the Beloved would fall into our embrace. God loves in the measure of man's own love. And the man who loves God must love all mankind, otherwise his love can not be perfect, it can not be divine. The babe is at its mother's breast." It is we in our ignorance enmeshed in the maya of this world forget God's presence and wander in darkness, which becomes more and more piercing, as we go further and further away from God. Says Eckhart: "To know God, we must become ignorant of ourselves and of all creatures." "Couldst thou annihilate thyself for a moment, thou would possess all that God is in Himself." This is complete renunciation which Eckhart speaks of.

In fact, there are seven stages to reach Godhead. The first is the *Valley of The Quest*. The man must hunger and thirst for God and when he does that he goes through purification. All his sins are washed off. He touches the way of "Supernal

Light," when he enters the *"Valley of Love."* It is the second stage in the journey of the soul. It may be called Dante's, *Earthly Paradise.* It is the mystic's first Illumination.

Then he passes to the *Valley of Knowledge* or Enlightenment, which brings him in communion with Truth. It is the third stage of the journey. He perceives God in all things. The next stage is the *Valley of Detachment,* when man has to do duty for the sake of duty without expectation of any return or reward. When he enters the *Valley of Unity,* after passing the Valley of Detachment, "naked Godhead" becomes the object of contemplation. He gets "Beatific Vision." His soul gets into ecstasies. But these ecstasies are still not firm. They are transient. He has to proceed to the sixth stage which is the *Valley of Amazement.* The medieval mystics called it "Divine Dark." His soul is plunged in darkness and bewilderment. But he soon gets out of it when he reaches the final goal, the *Valley of Annihilation* of Self. It is union with God or as Buddha would say, "the dewdrop slipping into the Ocean."

Says Eckhart, the spiritual pilgrim goes through the various valleys of experiences, because of his inner urge and because also that God is calling him. Man needs God but God also needs Man.

Eckhart calls complete annihilation of self as "decease." He says "When I am in this state, God brings forth His Son in me. Or conversely it is I who beget God a new in my soul. God has begotten me from eternity that I may be Father and beget

Him, who begot me."

Eckhart further argues that after getting to God, we must by His grace get rid of "God" and become one with the Essence, which is above God and above distinction — the Godhead.

Mortification of the flesh was considered by German and other mystics of medieval Europe, as a necessity for purification of the soul. They believed in practising poverty, for, to them poverty meant, "complete detachment from finite things." They practised chasity, which meant for them cleansing the soul of all desires, except love for God. They also practised complete obedience, which to them was the mortification of the will, complete indifference to life, and complete self-abandonment. To them, all that mattered was the love of God,— His purity, His goodness, His Beauty.

The following is a beautiful description of God, dwelling in a pure soul, by Eckhart:

"God is pure Good in Himself, therefore He would dwell nowhere but in a pure soul. There, He can pour Himself out; into that He can wholly flow. What is purity? It is that a man should have turned himself away from all creatures and have set his heart so entirely on the Pure Good that no creature is to him a comfort, that he has no desire for aught, creaturely, save so far as he may apprehend these in the Pure Good, which is God. And as little as the bright eye can endure aught foreign in it, so little can the pure soul bear anything in it, any stain that comes between it and God. To it all creatures are pure to enjoy, for it enjoyeth all creatures in God and God in all creatures."

Eckhart apart from Suso and others was quite justified, when he said, "All creatures are pure to enjoy." Asceticism does not necessarily mean mysticism. Asceticism is necessary for it leads to purification of the body, but as we have already said it should not be carried to such an extent as to destroy the body and bring untold physical suffering. The following passage from Evelyn Underhill's work, "Mysticism," would be read with interest, as it is replete with great beauty of thought:

"Whatever be the case of other deniers of the senses, it is true the soul of the great mystic, dwelling on the high levels of reality, his eye set on the transcendental world, is capable of combining with the perfection of detachment that intense and innocent joy in natural things as veils and vessels of the divine, which results from seeing all creatures in God and God in all creatures."

St. Theresa

Let us cast a glance at the life and spiritual experiences of St. Theresa, another remarkable mystic saint of mediaeval Europe. She was born in 1515 in a Spanish family of high repute. Her father was a man of devotion to God and he occupied his time mostly in works of charity. Theresa was one of the thirteen children of her parents, her father having married twice and she was born of his second wife. Her mother was a woman of delicate health. The child was brought up in a religious atmosphere. The home library contained books on knight errantry and lives of martyrs and saints. Theresa even when she was a girl read all these books; her mind was filled with romantic thoughts and her heart was lifted by the tales of the martyr heroes. A long illness at the age of sixteen made her resolute in her mind to renounce life. She entered a convent. For full twenty years, life to her was a struggle. Her fiery soul was tossed on the winds and whirlwinds of her own whims and passions. The cloistered life did not much appeal to her mind. Even when she prayed her mind wandered abroad. She was dissatisfied with life. But at last in 1554, came a new awakening in her soul. It was a new birth. Her father died and his death caused a great sadness in her heart.

One day she saw in a vision Christ at the oratory in wounded condition. The spectacle pierced her heart. She said that she felt that an angel had come with a lance tipped with fire, which was plunged into her heart. At the sight of the vision she fell into a trance and thereafter trances became common. She underwent a course of strong disciplinary treatment. As advised, she flogged herself daily with a whip of nettles. She wore haircloth plated with broken wires, which tore the skin and caused excruciating pain. One day she heard an angel saying. "Thou shalt have no more converse with men but with angels." It gave her infinite satisfaction and courage to put through her plan of bringing about reformation in the convents. She started her work at first in secrecy. She laid the foundation of many new convents and monasteries. She wrote her autobiography, which is a marvellous book of her spiritual experiences.

It is said, one day, in one of her visions, she saw her rosary snatched away and later on returned to her. To her mind it was not a rosary of ordinary beads but of resplendent diamonds. Her work took her out and she travelled mostly in rude carts without giving any thought to personal care or comfort. Such was the fire and enthusiasm contained in her frail body that she underwent all the privations and hardships with a cheerful mind. She died on 29th September 1582 and her body was interred at Alva.

A few months later on, the grave was unearthed and the coffin was opened. Some enthusiastic father cut her limb and it was found as fresh as ever. There was a sort of sweet fragrance hanging all over her body and the people were convinced that Theresa was a saint of a high order.

Ignatius Loyola

Ignatius Loyola, the founder of the Order of the Jesuits is a strong type of practical mystic. We are not concerned with the history of the movement of the Jesuits. We know what great amount of work this body has done in the interest of spreading

Christianity in all parts of the world. Barring their religious fanaticism, one would admire their zeal for spiritual life. We look upon Ignatius Loyola as a mystic, who indulged in meditative practices and considered meditation as the chief source of spiritual power. He used to say that a single hour of meditation had taught to him more truths of heavenly things than all the teachings of all the doctors put to-gether could have taught him. In this regard we are reminded of the four stages described by Swami Vivekananda in *Raja Yoga*, of *Samadhi*. He says, the first stage is that of concentration of the mind, on one point, usually by concentrating the mind on the tip of the nose. In the second stage of *samadhi*, the intellect ceases to function and there remains the satisfied sense of unity. In the third, there is no kind of satisfaction and instead a sort of indifference arises along with memory and self consciousness. In the fourth stage these three, viz, indifference, memory and self-consciousness are perfected and when one goes beyond it, he reaches a state when the meditator says, "There exists absolutely nothing. There are neither ideas nor absence of ideas."

The reader should excuse us for this digression but it is necessary in order to fully realize the conception of meditation, which is the keynote of all mysticism. The mystic leads the fullest life. To him the universe is not dead. It is a living presence.

St. John of the Cross

St. John of the Cross is a Spanish mystic of the 16th century. The following extracts from his teaching make very strange reading but they are of importance in as much as they give an idea of the extent of the suffering which the mystics bear voluntarily for the purpose of gaining perfect control of mind.

> "Let your soul turn always
>
> Not to what is most easy but to what is hardest;
>
> Not what tastes best, but to what is most distasteful
>
> Not to what most pleases, but to what disgusts;
>
> Not to matter of consolation, but to matter of desolation;
>
> Not to rest but to labour;
>
> Not to desire the more but the less;
>
> Not to aspire to what is highest and most precious but what is lowest and most contemptible;
>
> Not to will anything, but to will nothing;
>
> Not to seek the best in everything, but to seek the worst so that you may enter for the love of Christ into a complete destitution, a perfect poverty of spirit

> and an absolute renunciation of everything in the world.
>
> Embrace these practices with all the energy of your soul and you will find in a short time great delights and unspeakable consolation.
>
> Despise yourself and wish that others should despise you.
>
> Speak to your own disadvantage and desire that others did the same;
>
> Conceive a low opinion of yourself and find it good when others hold the same;
>
> To enjoy the taste of all things, have no taste for anything;
>
> Go through whatever experiences you have no taste for;
>
> To learn to know nothing, to go whither you are ignorant;
>
> To reach what you possess not, to go whither so ever you own nothing;
>
> To be what you are not, experience what you are not."

St. John sums up his whole conception of mysticism in the following cryptic lines:

> "When you stop at one thing, you cease to open yourself to the All

> For to come to the All, you must give up the All
> And if you should attain to owning the All You must own it designing nothing."

The Society of the Friends of God

In the beginning of the fourteenth century, in Germany, on account of political factions, people had no peace. The Church was corrupt and to add to their misery and suffering, natural calamities like flood, famine and pestilence swept the country. The Black Death in 1348 took a very heavy toll of life. In this state of agony, religion began to have a greater hold on the people.

An association called, the *Society of Friends of God* was formed. It was a society of mystics, headed by such men of renown and sacrifice as Henry Suso and Tauler. The followers of Eckhart were also participants in the movement. This society of intellectual and spiritual aspirants came into existence in Strasbourg. It soon spread in the neighbouring provinces and even beyond Switzerland. Its aim was to create a spiritual fervour among the people in the midst of the darkness of their life. And the result was a great outburst of transcendental activity. Members travelled from one place to another and exchanged their spiritual experiences. They corresponded with one another and sent books or relics to keep up the spiritual contact. This *Society of the Friends of God* had many features that were common with those of the Quakers.

Suso was a talented leader of this movement. We have already spoken of him in the earlier pages. He was a mystic of the most "exuberant Catholic type." He too like St. Theresa has written his autobiography, which is a narration of his spiritual experiences. It is a human document of great value. It is a record of his own joys and visions, pains and miseries revealed in rather a dramatic style.

The Society of the Friends of God had women members also, who took considerable part in its activities. They carried on a huge propaganda and created a beautiful religious atmosphere, which was the sorest need of the time. It lifted up the people from the slough of despondency and brought a religious revival of the highest type.

John Ruysbrock

John Ruysbrock (1293 — 1381) of Flanders deserves to be mentioned specifically as he is considered by several as one of the greatest mystics, the world has known. He was no doubt influenced by Eckhart and his mysticism is of similar nature, though in certain regards it differs from his inspirer and master. He is more practical and less speculative. He is chiefly concerned in devising means to attain union with God; to Eckhart the union is an ever present fact. Ruysbrock's mysticism gave birth to the formation of the Brethren of the Common Lot. Its members were not bound down to any monastic vows but they lived together in simplicity and piety, sharing everything in common like the old Church apostles.

George Fox

George Fox, the Founder of the "Society of Friends" was born at Drayton, in Leicestershire in July 1624. He was a son of a weaver and was apprenticed to a shoemaker. From his very childhood, he showed tendency for religion. But his father overlooked his natural inclination for higher life and made him an apprentice in a workshop. His employer dealt in cattle and wool also and the poor lad carried out his various duties, faithfully and loyally. One day, he was induced along with others to visit a public house. He returned home grief-stricken. He could not sleep. He heard the voice of God telling him, "Thou seest how young people go together into vanity and the old people into the earth; thou must forsake all, both young and old and keep out of all and be a stranger unto all."

To George Fox, this was a warning to avoid the shams of life and lead a holy, religious life, to think of God and God only, as He alone was the Reality and all else was "maya," to use the

language of the Hindu sanyasi. He left his home and tramped on foot from place to place. He became an itinerant preacher. Bitter trials and tribulations became the order of the day. He was persecuted and harassed. But he bore his sufferings and hardships with a heroic heart. There was an inward joy in him that helped him in all the external struggles and hardships. He said, "I had intermissions and was sometimes brought into such heavenly joy that I thought I had been in Abraham's bosom." He saw in his visions the image of Christ enter into his heart. Revelations came to him one after another and it strengthened him to face the opposition that the Presbyterians and others raised against him. He was opposed to Church doctrine. What he believed in was the doctrine of the heart. He was a sincere and earnest preacher and a follower of God. He considered conventions and customs as shams of life. What he taught was that man must give heed to the inner voice; he must look within, not look without. He must be guided by the inner light and not by the scriptures alone. He was against the churchianity as preached from the pulpits. He was a heavenly-minded soul, whose heart was deeply merged in the ocean of God. In a way he was a true mystic and a zealous worker, who courted imprisonment several times rather than that he should give up his own convictions. He succeeded in laying the foundation of a great movement which is known as "Society of Friends" or Quakers. They are a body which still exercises a considerable stable influence upon Christian society chiefly in England. Opposed to war, litigation and conventions, they form a body of mystics in the truest sense of the word.

We are told that in the beginning in the time of Fox, his followers showed such religious excitement, that they were accused of indulging in excesses and eccentricities which were against all decency of life. They would strip off their clothes and go naked in processions. They would force themselves into hysterical swoons and mystical raptures.

This simplicity and purity of the Quakers, their love for truth and righteousness, their submission to the will of God under all circumstances, their avoidance of all kinds of pleasures especially theatres and dances, their opposition to oaths and ceremonies — these form the mental make up of the great society, which Fox by his own example of austerity and sincerity was able to build up.

Fox had to undergo many trials but he was dauntless and firm in his mind. The illumination of the soul came to him as in the case of other mystics after a good deal of purification and mortification. Fox's journal for the year 1647, gives a graphic picture of this inward struggle. He says, "Thus in the deepest miseries and in the greatest sorrows and temptations that many times beset me, the Lord in His mercy did keep me. I found that there were two thirsts in me, the one after the creatures to get help and strength there; and the other after the Lord, the creator. It was so with me, that there seemed to me two pleadings in me. One day when I was walking solitarily abroad and had come home, I was wrapped into the love of God, so that I could not but admire the greatness of His love. While I was in that condition it was opened unto me by the eternal light and power and I saw clearly therein — But O! then did I see my troubles, trials and temptations more clearly than ever I had done."

Fox was a man of superhuman vitality, which can be gauged by the enormous quantity of his work, — a giant in spirit. The Quaker movement started by Fox was an outbreak of genuine mysticism more or less of the "Friends of God", founded by the German mystics like Suso and Eckhart in the mediaeval ages in Europe which we have already described in the foregoing pages.

4

SRI RAMANA MAHARSHI

(*The Sage of Arunachala*)

In the galaxy of saints and sages that India has produced in the recent times, — Sri Ramakrishna Paramahamsa, Swami Vivekananda, Sri Aurobindo Ghosh and others — Sri Ramana, the Sage of Arunachala, occupies an honoured place. It is the proud distinction of India, that this country has produced more saints and sages than any other country in the world. It would not be wrong to say that India is the cradle of spirituality and its greatest contribution is its most welcoming effort to spiritualise the world by its spiritual philosophy. There is no greater advocate of peace in the war-shattered world to-day than India, which is due to its innate spirituality. Its spiritual stalwarts have raised India high in the estimation of the world.

Venkataramana was born on 30th December, 1879 in a village about seventy miles from Madura, in South India. He was born of happy parents and was destined to become a great sage. He was a strange lad. When put to school, he showed no inclination for studies. He was more fond of meditation than of school work. One day, he was rebuked by his elder brother who was his guardian after the death of his father for not attending to his lessons. He was grievously hurt. He made up his mind to leave his house in search of his Father.

We know of several instances of persons leaving their homes in their tender years in response to the inner urge to seek God. St. Francis of Assissi was rebuked by his father for lifting a bale of cloth from his shop and selling it off to get money for repairing a church building in ruins. The boy was so annoyed that he left the parental roof. True to the Biblical teaching, he left his father's house, without a coin in his pocket and with very little clothing on his body in search of his Father trusting in Providence to guide and help him. He lived to become the founder of the great St. Franciscan Order.

Similarly we are told of George Fox, the founder of the Quaker Movement, that he left his father's house, at a very young age, in absolute penury. He had intense faith in God, whom he loved with all his heart and soul. He was subjected to harsh persecutions. But he was made of sterner stuff. He met all the opposition with perfect equanimity of mind.

Sri Ramana had once heard the name of Arunachala. That name had so inflamed his soul, that when his brother taunted him he thought it was a good opportunity to put into practice the dream of his life to run away and become a

Sanyasin. Sometimes on the mere utterance of certain names or on seeing certain objects, the mind gets enkindled and the soul's craving is excited for things that are transcendental. It had so happened in the case of the boy, Venkataraman, when the word "Arunachala" fell upon his ears.

Venkataraman's brother had given him Rs. 5/- to pay his college fee. He had no money of his own. He therefore took three rupees to pay his third class railway fare from his village to the railway station nearest to the temple of Arunachala and returned the balance to his brother leaving a note behind. This note written in Tamil has a mystical significance and it is necessary to give an exact English translation of it.

"In search of my Father.

"I have, according to His command, started from this place. On a virtuous enterprise indeed, has this embarked. Therefore, for this act, none need grieve nor trace this out, nor need money be spent,

Thus,

Your college fees yet not paid.

Rs. 2/- are herewith."

The boy writes the letter beginning with "I". He ends the letter without any signature of his own. Why is it so? It appears to us that the letter was written under divine inspiration and it was a forerunner of his own great teaching viz., that in every individual there are two "I"s. The one "I" is individualistic. It seeks his own self. This "I" has to be submerged and the other "I" is the universal "I". It is the Real Self which has to be revealed. In not signing the letter, he was indicating the process of submergence of his personality into the egoless state, so necessary for the realization of the Real Self.

The first step necessary in Self-realization is to acquire the habit of complete fearlessness. Death creates generally fear in man. The boy had therefore resolved to get over this fear aspect by imagining himself in the clutches of death. He had meditated upon his body as melting away and he had imagined the pain and anguish of such physical disruption. This is how he had conquered the fear complex before he had left the house.

Sri Ramana like Sri Ramakrishna Paramahamsa had very little of Scriptural knowledge. Except the book of "Periyapuranam", which is a biography of some well known saints, he had read nothing. It was such a lad who was hunting for his Father's House in Eternity.

When the boy reached the Temple of Arunachala, in Tiruvannamalai which was the gamut of his aspiration, completely exhausted in body, having tramped a long distance on foot, without adequate food and water, his mind was so full of joy that he gave expression to his inner feelings of delight in the following magnificent manner:

"O Lord, obedient to Thy call,
Here have I come, deserting all,

No boon I ask, no loss bemoan
Take me in and make me Thine Own."

He now makes his home in the forest of Arunachala. He forgets his mother, the dearest living soul to him. Is it not said in the Bible: "He that loveth father or mother more than Me is not worthy of Me".

(St. Matthew X, 37)

His subliminal intuition tells him that the best way to realize God is to lose the sense of individual possession and affection. Is it not said in the Bible, "Whosoever shall save his life shall lose it; and whosoever shall lose his life for My sake shall find it?"

(St. Mathew XVI, 25)

Sri Ramana takes to meditation. Except a small bit of cloth, which he wears as a cod-piece he discards everything. He is content and happy in his semi-nude condition. The cod-piece, he wears, is not so much for the purpose of maintaining decency, but as a symbol of his vow of austerity and *tyaga* (renunciation). It is a symbol of his renouncing everything in life, especially sex. He belongs to no cult, no school of thought. He recognises no *guru*. He follows no rules, no conventions. He is independent of all paraphernalia. They have no place in the economy and exigency of his spiritual life. God alone is his lodestar and he dedicates his all to that great Being, Lord of the Universe. The world appears to him as a shadow. It can take nothing from him; it can give nothing to him. He turns his attention inwards and there he finds the key to the secrets of the universe.

The great Buddha got enlightenment by meditating under the shade of the Bodhi-tree, after he had spent six long years in the vain attempt to find Truth by the practice of austerity and external renunciation. But Sri Ramana got Self-realization without any effort. In fact, it is one of his great teachings that efforts are obstacles in the path of God-realization. This may appear to us to be too paradoxical and nonsensical on the face of it. But there is a depth of meaning in this statement. When one forgets himself in the love of God and his mind is fixed on God, hour after hour, day after day, week after week and month after month; when his mind is saturated and soaked in the waters of divinity, it is evident, that in such a state of mind, whatever is done or achieved is no effort. All his actions become spontaneous and effortless. There is no struggle, no strain. He becomes dumb to the sense of pleasure and pain. Within him, there is joy regardless of the outward condition of his body.

We are told that when Sri Ramana used to go into meditative trances, the school urchins used to throw stones at him and mock at him. But their mischievous pranks made not the least impression upon him. The equanimity of his mind was not the least disturbed. He generally was so rapt up in his meditative mind that he hardly cared for food. He had no fear of snakes and cobras which were plentiful in the forest where he meditated. If he was given food, he took it, but he never went in search of it. Seeing this situation several persons became his immediate followers. They undertook to attend upon him by turns in the forest cave where he had made his abode. He lived for years in this manner unmindful of rain and sun, fog and winter. Several times it was noticed that snakes and cobras were on his body but he was quite indifferent and they injured him not. Ants and worms, mosquitoes and bees continuously pestered him. His naked body was the target of their onslaughts and it was covered with ulcers. But he was quite indifferent to it. Is it not said in the *Gita*?

"Whosoever, by comparison with himself, sees the same every where, O Arjuna, be it pleasure or pain, he is deemed the highest yogin".

(Discourse VI, 32)

We are told by the author of Self-Realization, that so deep were the sores made by the stings of the bees and insects that "their scars are visible on his body even at the present day after the lapse of more than forty years."

It is said that he practised *vairagya* to such an extent that even the most elementary needs of his body were neglected. His nails grew so long that his hands became useless. His hair became matted and was full of dirt. When he used to go into *samadhi,* he remained unwashed for days and weeks together. The external world ceased to exist for him. To one who had realized Self, what mattered, what happened to his body. An ascetic of ascetics, a *sanyasin* of *sanyasins* we do not know of any other instance of such extreme renunciation.

Ramana's body grew emaciated with constant fasting. His mind also became so tame, that it seemed that it had ceased to function. He had no conception of time, whether it was morning, noon or evening. He had ceased to reckon days, weeks or months. Such a person in the West would have been literally transferred to a mental hospital for pyscho-therapeutic treatment.

Both the Eastern and Western countries have produced spiritual stalwarts, who have made a mark in life. Suso, the great German mystic, St. Theresa, St. Francis of Assissi, Ignatius Loyola, George Fox, St. John of the Cross, Meister Eckhart, William Blake — these are some of the flowers of Western Mysticism. It is creditable that Europe could produce mystical saints and seers, as mentioned above when the general attitude of the people toward life was more materialistic than spiritual. The materialistic tendency of European civilization is reflected in the writings of such authors as George Goodwin whose book, "The Great Mystics" is nothing but a denunciation of mysticism. It is not surprising that such authors living in the midst of materialistic morass should denounce mysticism and consider mystical experiences as mental aberrations and mystics as self-deluding lunatics indulging in pathological voluptuousness. In this respect the West has much to learn from the East, particularly India, which is a home of saints and seers.

The disciples of Sri Ramana call him "Bhagwan". "Bhagwan" means God. Is he a God in the shape of man? In India, the guru is placed as high as God. It is Sri Ramana's own teaching also. He himself is very humble and does not claim himself to be superior to or higher than any person in life. But his teaching is that God and Guru are really the same. According to him the Guru's grace is the same as God's grace.

Sri Ramana became conscious of the great blissful condition he had entered into on the very day, he reached the temple of Arunachala, when he was hardly seventeen years old. His is an unparalleled record of having attained Self-realization at such an early age, and at a flash, without the guidance of any *Guru* and without having undergone the apprenticeship of a regular sanyasin's life. He was installed into the inner regions of eternal bliss straight from the school without any external training or guidance, which is so very necessary in the ordinary course of things. He is an exceptional case of God's Grace having descended upon him in such an unparalleled manner. He became an *Avadhuta*, at a very tender age. This Sanskrit word "Avadhuta" contains four syllables and expresses the following meaning:

The first letter "A" stands for the Sanskrit word *aksharatva,* meaning imperishability. The second syllable "va" stands for "*varenyatva*" meaning the acme of perfection. The third syllable "du" stands for "*dhuta-samsara-bhandhana*"meaning the breaking of the bonds of *samsara*. The fourth and the last syllable "ta" stands for "*tattvamasyedi eakshyatva,*" meaning Realization of Truth viz., THAT THOU ART.

Salvation is the goal of life. In the instance of Sri Ramana, as we have already pointed out, it was achieved when he was still in his teens, without any effort. Usually it requires years of patient practice to rise above the body and mind consciousness, so very necessary to gain salvation. But to Sri Ramana, Self-Realization came like a shot. He became conscious of Self in everything and everywhere. All beings sentient and insentient were alike to him. To him no problems existed. He was utterly indifferent to the exterior world. He has reached the stage of *Sahaja Samadhi,* that is, he was all the time merged in the Ocean of Eternal Bliss. He was *Sat Chit Ananda.*

When yogis and mystics go into trances it is for a short time. They get glimpses of the eternal light but as soon as they return from their *samadhi* they no longer experience that transendent bliss. The egoless state of *Sahaja Samadhi* is very rarely attained. Historically, Gautama Buddha and Sri Sankaracharya are said to have attained this state of imperishable bliss.

It is said, one should be a saint to understand a saint. A large section of people consider Maharshi Ramana as only a holy man and not a sage or God-realized man. They argue, "He eats and drinks and sleeps like an ordinary man. He does all that is expected of an ordinary man. When he speaks, it is in the ordinary terms of "I", "you" and "he". There is nothing strange in him. He is not able to do miracles. They contend that he is conscious of both mind and body. He cannot therefore be classified as a sage or a God-realized man."

This is obviously a harsh judgment based on ignorance. Those who are still in the bondage of body and mind are not likely to judge correctly. People have a false notion that miracle working is a sign of spirituality. To a Self-realized man there is no such thing as a miracle. Miracles are ordinary things to him. The real object of life is Self-Realization. A *Raja Yogi* can perform miracles. We know of many instances of *yogis* having done that. Buddha came across an Indian *yogi* who had done meditation for a number of years and had attained the power of walking on waters. Buddha said to him: "You have meditated for twenty years and in return you have achieved the power of crossing the river. I could do it by spending an anna or half on the hire of a seat in a boat which would safely take me to the other shore. Do you call this a great achievement, which is worth not more than an anna?"

The power to do miracles is inherent in every God-realized person but it is seldom used or exercised for it is his mission to bring men nearer to God by infiltrating into their minds that the world is a delusion and that the true and lasting happiness lies only in achieving the egoless state, when the consciousness of both the body and the mind is submerged.

Sri Ramana is a sage because he shows us from his personal experience what is real and what is not real. His humility, his perception of unity in nature, his conviction of non-separateness in life, his egoless state, his love for all alike, his indifference to praise or blame, his equal treatment of every one, whether a saint or a sinner, his treatment of the world as unreal, "reducing the unreal to unreality and causing the ONE REAL SELF to shine'— these are some of the traits of a sage which are amply seen in the person and character of Sri Ramana. Distinctions of any nature do not enter into the purview of a sage. "The equal vision of the sage is just the recognition that the One Self who is consciousness is present in all that appears."

The sage does not look at the world as others do. He rejects the unreal part of the world and accepts only the Substratum, which is the formless, pure consciousness, the Self.

When a man realizes Self, the doors of all knowledge open out to him. It is not necessary that one endowed with spiritual and scriptural knowledge alone can realise Self. Neither Sri Ramana nor Sri

Ramakrishna Paramahamsa were students of any religious literature. They were quite ignorant of their Scriptures. But both of them have given their own gospels. The heart is the seer of the Self. What is wanted in Self-realization is the dissolution of the mind into the heart.

The activities of the sage are different from ours. We think that we are doers. But the sage does not think so. To speak in the words of the author of *Maha Yoga*: "What seems to us to be his (sage's) activities are not therefore really his. Being egoless and mindless, he does not will those actions. The self same power by which the activities are prompted and sustained is behind those of the Sage also, with this difference that while the ignorant think they themselves are the doers, the Sage does not think so. He acts automatically, as a sleepy child eats when roused and fed by its mother. If any agency is to be ascribed to somebody, let it be rather ascribed to God, than to the sage, because while God is in one point of view the regulator of the world, the Sage has nothing to do with the world. In truth, that is the Egoless State, both are identical, neither is an agent, because neither is other than the Real Self, which is ONE."

(Pages 230 and 231)

The same author in order to prove that the Sage is mindless and egoless i.e., his actions are not the outcome of desire or will, tells us of an incident in the life of Sri Ramana. Once the Sage was passing by the hill of Arunachala, when accidentally his foot fell upon a cluster of bees which were hiding underneath a dense foliage. The offended creatures settled upon the offending leg and the Sage remained motionless. It was a spontaneous action. He allowed the bees to spend their wrath upon his leg, saying to the leg, "Take the consequences of your action."

The sage is pure consciousness and therefore mindless. He is free. For him there are no duties, no rights, no regrets. They are meaningless words to him. He is actionless. We are reminded of the following lines in the *Gita*.

"Renouncing all actions by thought and self-controlled, the embodied on rests happily in the nine gated city, neither at all acting nor causing to act."

(Discourse V, 13)

When one sits at the feet of the Master, he feels that he is surrounded with an atmosphere of surpassing joyousness. He feels as if he were in a state of trance. He forgets to put to the Sage whatever questions he may have prepared at home for reply by the sage. In fact, he automatically gets a reply to them by himself. He sits in his presence in absolute silence. His mind, soul and heart are as if it were glued together in a motionless state of transcendental joy. Can there be a more convincing proof of the fascination which the sage can exercise upon our inner self?

There is a story related that once thieves entered into, the Ashram of Ramana. He welcomed them to take away whatever they liked but not to harm any one. This did not satisfy the robbers. They savagely beat the dogs and some of the inmates. Sri Ramana was also not spared. They could get hold of very little money, as there was so little. What naturally can be expected of Sanyasins who live from hand to mouth, wedded to a life of poverty? The next day the police was sent for by the inmates of the ashram to make a search for the thieves who had molested them and bolted away. But Sri Ramana entreated them not to pursue the matter and to give up the search. He wanted the thieves to be left alone. All he said was that they were misguided persons blinded by ignorance. His mild retort to the disciples was: "Sometimes your teeth suddenly bite your tongue. Do you knock out the teeth in consequence?" What words of wisdom? What a sense of non-separateness? Such words can emanate only from one who is in tune with the Infinite.

Sri Ramana, to our mind has all those qualifications of a sage as described in the *Gita* and we give below the relevant text:

"Supreme Bliss verily comes to the *Yogin,* whose mind is quite tranquil, whose passion is quieted, who has become Brahman, who is blemishless."

"Thus always keeping the self steadfast, the yogin, freed from sins, attains with ease to the infinite bliss of contact with the Supreme Brahman."

"The Self abiding in all beings, and all beings abiding in the self, sees he whose self has been made steadfast by *yoga,* who every where sees the same."

"He who sees Me every where and sees everything in Me, to him I vanish not, nor to Me does he vanish."

"Whoso intent on unity, worships Me, who abides in all beings, that *yogin* dwells in Me, whatsoever his mode of life."

"Whoso, by comparison with himself, sees the same everywhere, O Arjuna, be it pleasure or pain, he is deemed the highest *yogin.*"

(Discourse VI, 27–32)

Sri Ramana is called the silent sage. He practises "mauna" (silence) for he considers silence as more eloquent than speech. When he speaks, which is at very rare intervals, words of wisdom fall from his lips. No wonder, Paul Brunton, the author of "A Search in Secret India" and various other books, which have made his name famous throughout the world for his acquaintance with spiritual knowledge gained by his having contacted Indian *yogis* and *sanyasins,* was a sceptic at first, when he saw Sri Ramana for the first time at Arunachala. His various visits to him convinced him that Sri Ramana was a God-realized man and he has paid the highest tributes to him. He says: "I journeyed Eastwards in search of yogis and their hermetic knowledge. I can only say that in India I found my faith restored. Not so long ago, I was among those who regard God as a hallucination of human fancy, spiritual truth as a mere nebula and providential justice as a confession of infantile idealists. I, too was somewhat impatient of those who construct theological paradises and who then confidently show round with an air of being God's estate agents. I had nothing but contempt for what seemed to be the futile, fanatical efforts of uncritical believers. This faith was restored in the only one way a sceptic would have it restored, not by argument, but by the witness of an overwhelming experience. And it was a jungle sage, an unassuming hermit who had formerly lived for twenty years in a mountain cave, who promoted this vital change in my thinking. It is quite possible that he could not pass a matriculation examination, yet I am not ashamed to record in the closing chapters of this book my deep indebtedness to this man."

(A Search in Secret India)

The following quotation from another of Paul Brunton's books called, "The Secret Path" gives us a vivid description of the impression made by the sage upon his soul.

"The hour of our first meeting is still graven on my memory. I met him unexpectedly. He made no attempt at formal introduction. For an instant those sybelline eyes gazed into mine but all the stained earth of my past and the white flowers that had begun to spring upon it, were alike seen during the one twinkle of the bell of time. There in that seated being was a great impersonal force that read the scales of my life with better sight than I could ever hope do. I had slept in the scented bed of Aphrodite and he knew it; I had lured the gnomes of thought to mine for strange enchanted gold in the depths of my spirit; he knew that too, felt too, that if I could follow him into his mysterious places of thought, all my miserliness would drop away, my resentment turn to toleration and I would understand life, not merely grumble at it. He interested me much despite the fact that his wisdom was not of a kind which is easily apparent and despite the strong reserve which encircled him. He broke his habitual silence only to answer questions upon such recondite topics as the nature of man's soul, the mystery of God, the strange powers which lie unused in the human mind and so on but when he did venture to speak, I used to sit enthralled as I listened to his soft voice under burning tropic sun or pale crescent moon. For authority was vested in that calm voice and inspiration gleamed in those luminous eyes. Each phrase that fell from his lips seemed to contain some precious fragment of essential truth. The theologians of stiffer century taught the doctrine of man's original sin; but the adept taught the doctrine of man's original goodness.

"In the presence of the Sage, one felt security and inward peace. The spiritual radiations which emanated from him were all penetrating. I learnt to recognise in his person the sublime truth which he taught, while I was no less hushed into reverence by his incredibly sainted atmosphere. He possessed a deific personality which defies description. I might have taken short hand notes of the discourses of this sage. I might even print the record of his speech but the most important part of his utterances, the subtle and silent flavour of his spirituality which emanate from him can never be reported. If therefore I burn literary incense before his bust, it is a mere fraction of the tribute I ought to pay to him.

"One could not forget that wonderful pregnant smile of his with its hint of wisdom and peace won from suffering and experience. He was the most understanding man I have ever known; you could always be sure of some words from him that would smoothen your way a little and that always verified what your deepest feeling told you.

"And yet in its settled moment, his face bore an expression of deep melancholy; still it was resigned melancholy; not the bitter rebellious kind one often sees — you know that in some period of his past he had suffered some inexpressible agony."

"The words of the sage still flame out in my memory like beacon lights. 'I pluck golden fruit from rare meetings with wise men' wrote trans-Atlantic Emerson in his diary and it is certain that I plucked whole basketfuls during my talks with this man. Our best philosophers of Europe could not hold a candle to him." (*The Secret Path*)

God is all joyousness. Does the face of Sri Ramana give a picture of resigned melancholy? We don't think so. Paul Brunton's impression of the sage's 'resigned melancholy' may be correct or not correct. But one should not judge by external appearances. Our own experience is, his face shows the serenity of a still lake without even the twitter of a ripple on its smooth surface. Such majesty of look, such deep serenity, such sparkling eyes, such beautiful radiance at least the writer has not seen in the course of his whole life in any one else. How can his look be emblematical of melancholy, when the sole concern of the sage is to radiate joy and happiness, which he intensifies without exhaustion for the benefit of his innumerable devotees.

God is all love. God is all peace. God is all beauty. God is all grace. God is all beatitude and whether the sage has a melancholy look or a radiant face, what matters is, not what he looks but what spell of happiness he is able to cast upon his votaries from the inner treasure of his spirituality.

Sri Ramana has transformed so many lives and given them the desired "moksha." He gave *moksha* to his own mother, when, afflicted with the dire calamity of the bereavement of her sons, she came to Sri Ramana and made her abode with him in the jungle, cooking for him and his immediate followers, leading a Spartan life of strenuous labour in the solitude of the mountain cave, completely detached from the glamour of the outside world and devoted in soul and spirit to Sri Ramana, whom she now looked upon not as her son, but the Lord and Master of her spirit, her very God.

Let us take stock of Sri Ramana's teachings. When a man goes to the sage, the first thing the latter asks him, is, whether he has enquired of himself, what he is. In ancient Greece, the motto displayed prominently at the Delphic Temple was, "KNOW THYSELF." These two words have a deep inner significance. The secret of nature lies within our heart. How many of us care to look within in search of Truth. We are so much carried away by external appearances that we hardly spare any time for internal investigation for self analysis or self scrutiny. We allow ourselves to be swayed by our bodily desires and passions and become easy victims to fear. We believe that the world is real. We believe that our mind is everything and that it plays an important part in the panorama of life. But this world, this body and this mind are all delusions.

Intuitively all of us desire happiness and this desire for happiness is natural because there is hidden within us the divine spark. It is the Self. To know the Self is the goal of life. How to know it, is a question.

When we are in deep sleep we are happy. We do not realise then that we have a body and mind. This fact should guide us that body consciousness and mind consciousness are obstacles in the path of Self-realization.

We look at the world and think that is real, because we see it with the aid of our sense organs.

We mistake a snake for a piece of rope. We mistake the mirage in the desert for a sheet of water. In order to understand what is real and what is not real, we must try to comprehend and understand what makes a thing real. The barber throws away the hair he cuts from a man's head for it has no value. It is dirt. Non-self is that dirt. It is of no value. We need not therefore discuss Non-Self, which is unreal. What we have to do is to get at the root of things to understand the real Reality.

The ancients used the system of elimination. *Neti-neti*, not this, not that and they eventually by the process of elimination and discarding arrived at the ultimate Truth. That is Real which is eternal, indivisible, imperishable, formless, colourless and beyond the conception of time, space and causality. Reality is that which is neither dependent nor interdependent upon anything in nature. The Absolute is the Self and the Self is the Absolute. Reality is pure Consciousness.

The world is therefore not real in the true sense of the word. We should not therefore be carried away by the external appearances and circumstances. Even our present day science has come to realise that the world is not composed of mere matter. The atomic theory has been thoroughly exploded. The scientists have discovered that an atom could be divided into protons and electrons, positrons and neutrons, which means that matter when reduced to extremity is not matter but spirit or energy. Matter is the material form of spirit. It is the invisible that is eternal, changeless, timeless, spaceless. The Invisible is the Real. The visible that is subject to the conditions of time, space and causality is unreal.

Einstein's theory of Relativity has further thrown a flood of light on our modern scientific problems. He says that time and space should not be considered as separate entities, as they do not exist separately. He suggests that the combination of the two, namely time and space i.e., time-space be considered as an entity. This again is purely a hypothetical statement; it is a statement assumed to understand physical phenomena. No one can directly experience such a thing as time-space.

Time, space and causality are mere creatures of the mind. It is Sri Ramana's teaching that if we want to realise the Self, which alone is Real we must rise above the body and mind consciousness. There are two "I"s in every one. The first "I" is the individualistic, egoistic "I" which thinks in the terms of transitory gains. It is unreal. the second "I" is the real "I", the true Self, which is universal, Absolute. The body is subject to destruction. Body consciousness is not an aid but an obstacle in the path of God-realization. We have to reach the Self by the channel of the Spirit and not matter. Body is matter and though it has to perform certain functions in life, no importance should be given to it. A life of disirelessness and austerity is necessary to gain the inward awareness.

But the greater difficulty is of the control of the

mind. Self-realization can be achieved only when the egoless stage is reached. Says the sage:

"When the sense of "I am the body" arises, then the notion of "you" and "he" also arises but when the quest is of the truth, underlying the "I" and the "I" sense is put an end to, then the notion of "you" and "he" also ceases, that which then shines as the sole remainder is the true Self."

The ego sense is our primary ignorance. It confounds forms with the Real Self and it thus limits the Real Self. The sage says: "If the Self be with the form, then the world and God would be so too. But if the Self be formless, then how and by whom are forms to be seen? Is the spectacle ever other than the seeing eye is? The Real "I" is just the Self. It is infinite consciousness, formless, worldless."

Forms are creations of our ego-sense and the ego has its foundation in ignorance.

What is then required is the light of true knowledge. The world is a *maya*, as our ancient rishis have so unmistakenly demonstrated to us and ego — the truant mind — is the Macbeth in the tragedy of the human life.

Mind is the organ of the soul. The soul gets strengthened as the mind evolves and thinks of good thoughts. One need not classify mind into higher and lower mind. But if the mind becomes higher and higher, it will eventually get itself absorbed into the ocean of eternity. When the individual "I" is dissolved into the universal "I" the Self is revealed. There is only one Supreme Being and none else has any separate existence. As the Scripture says:

"There is no seer, hearer, thinker or knower apart from this Being. There is none but He that sees, hears, thinks or knows. "Thou Art that," "I am the Reality."

When some one asked the sage to clarify the meaning of the phrase "Thou Art That" he gave a very beautiful explanation. He said: "Thou art not the body, nor the senses, nor the mind, nor the vital force, nor the ego. Thou art That, which shines as the pure "I AM". By the quest of Self, the mind is utterly extinguished in the heart and the world ceases to be seen."

The teaching of Sri Ramana that this world is a *maya* synchronises with the teaching of the *Gita*. Lord Krishna says:

"All the creatures are in Me. I am not in them, (in Truth) they are not in Me, such is my divine maya.

(Discourse IX, 4)

He who is in the quest of Truth must rise above body consciousness and mind consciousness. The most turbulent and relentless enemy in the Path of Self-Realization is the ego. It is the Ahreman, the Satan, the Macbeth, the arch deceiver of human peace and happiness. The egoless state is the highest state. Nay, it is the natural state, for it is the birthright of every person to become a God. Did not Christ say:

"That they all may be one; as Thou, Father, art in me, and I in Thee, that they also may be one in us: that the world may believe that Thou hast sent me."

(St. John XVII, 21)

The only way to destroy the ego sense is to concentrate upon the fact that Self alone exists and all else is a delusion. Complete surrender to the Real Self comes when we take the path of devotion which ultimately leads to the path of " jnana."

Swami Vivekananda says: "The greatest help to spiritual life is meditation. In meditation we divest ourselves of all material conditions and feel our divine nature. We do not depend upon any external help in meditation. The touch of the soul can paint the brightest colour even in the dingiest places; it can cast a fragrance, over the vilest thing; it can make the wicked divine, — and all enmity, all selfishness is effaced. The less the thought of the body, the better. For it is the body, that drags us down. It is attachment, identification, which makes us miserable. That is the secret. To think that I am the spirit and not the body and the whole of the universe with all its relations, with all its good and all its evil, is but as a series of paintings, scenes on a canvas, of which I am the witness." (Swami Vivekananda's Realization and Its Methods — pages 35 and 36.)

The above passage gives in a nutshell the whole of the *Advaita* philosophy, of which Swami

Vivekananda was a staunch advocate and Sri Ramana though he had not studied Shankara's commentaries and was not versed even in the *Gita* and other Scriptures, intuitively practised these very things which were taught by the *rishis* of old in India. He attained to nature's secret by identifying his self with the Universal Self.

The soul is free. Sri Ramana's life indicates the fact, how one can achieve the highest spiritual perfection by one's own self without the intercession of any one. Of course, it is an exceptional case. But at the same time it shows that it is possible for a human being to attain to the highest state of spirituality without the aid of any one whatsoever by one's own efforts. The soul in Sri Ramana's case was his *guru*. As Swami Vivekananda says: "There is no help for you outside of yourself, you are the creator of the universe." The silkworm, to take the analogy of Swami Vivekananda, builds a cocoon round itself, to save itself. Our body and our bodily desires and the mind and the attachments of the mind are the silkworm's cocoon. We have to annihilate both the body and the mind. When the cocoon is broken, the beautiful butterfly emerges. When the body is discarded and the mind is controlled, our soul becomes free, like the butterfly.

The following quotation from the talks of the sage will be found very instructive:

"Religion, whether it is Christianity, Buddhism, Hinduism, Theosophy or any other kind of "Ism" or "Sophy" or system can only take us to one point where all religions meet and no further."

"That one point where all religions meet is the realization not in some mystical sense but in the most wordly, most literal and every day sense — and the more wordly and practical the better — of the fact, GOD IS EVERYTHING AND EVERYTHING IS GOD."

"God is infinite and therefore existence and non-existence are merely His counterparts. Not that I wish to say that God is made up of definite component parts. It is hard to be comprehensive when talking of God. True knowledge comes from within, not from without and true knowledge is not intellectual knowing but actual literal Being of one's self as God i.e., through the most practical, most literal and actual realisation of the fact that God is everything and everything is God."

The ashram where the sage lives is situated in one of the most enchanting spots of nature. There are beautiful temples engraved in stone and marble round about the Hill of the Beacon Light which is said to be more ancient than the Himalayas, the chief source of attraction to the Hindu pilgrims. They come here in their thousands at the time of the annual festival bringing with them their offerings of ghee and oil which are poured in the tunnel made on the top surface of the hoary hill. The oil is lighted and the whole mountain blazes out in a terrific red flame, throwing its light all around, presenting a picturesque and soul stirring sight. It is said that the Beacon Light lasts for a number of days. Fire is held as a very sacred emblem both among the Hindus and Parsis. Parsis worship fire, as they hold it the very embodiment of God — Light and Purity.

We can imagine the enthusiasm of the pilgrims and their joy at the sight of the gorgeous flame bursting and leaping out from the mountain top in all its red glory, illuminating the whole countryside.

But greater than the attraction of the Hill of the Beacon Light is the attraction of the Sage himself. In Madras the people are more religious minded than in any other part of India. The authorities of the *ashram* keep an open door of hospitality to all comers. The *ashram* is situated in a lovely spot of nature, surrounded by hills and mountains and sheltered in a thick foliage of tall trees, bedecked with exquisite greenery so pleasing to the eye and the soul. The buildings are kept clean and tidy and the comforts of the visitors are well looked after.

Sri Ramana is a tall person, a little aged in look and somewhat emaciated in body, with eyes that penetrate your very soul and read your inner self like a book. Being a man of silence he hardly opens his mouth. He sits on a raised dais in the hall where congregate visitors who squat on the ground at the feet of the Master. The Sage would be seen sitting morning, noon and evening, rapt in deep thought, all hours of the day, except when he goes out on a solitary walk in the woods by the side of the projecting hill. In the hushed silence of the hall, one feels a peculiar notion that he is no more in the mundane world, but in some spirit land full of peace and tranquility. There is exultation in the air and an unending wave of peace and harmony, so enchanting to the soul.

Each one enters into the hall with a quiver in his heart. He prostrates before the figure of the holy man, who is all naked except for a loin cloth and takes his seat on the floor. He is immediately submerged in a wave of thoughts and his mind is entranced in the pindrop silence of the hall. In that arena of deep and sombre silence, each one raises questions to himself to clear his doubts. The questions are put mentally and by a strange working of nature they are automatically answered.

I felt, sitting in that silent crowd of devotees and visitors as if my heart's flame had been lit and that my soul was ready for its flight. There came upon me the feeling of universal harmony — a sort of rapture to be united with all, for, is not GOD EVERYTHING AND EVERYTHING GOD? I felt that the greater Light of God was vibrating in that hall of pindrop silence and that the minds and hearts of those sitting in that sombre room, linked in silence, were being cemented to work for one end and purpose viz., to serve God and God alone, for is He not the only Reality? Who can describe the feeling of tranquility, the transcendental joy, the transformation of the mundane into the ethereal?

I had the opportunity of exchanging a few words with the Sage, both in the hall and outside. The look of sweetness he gave, the gleam in his eyes, the wave of his hands as if to say that he knew all for which I had come and the expression of the thought that the cherished hope in my heart will be fulfilled, without making any tangible mention of it, but all the same in a very subtle but determined manner — how can the memory of that fragrant, pregnant hour be ever forgotten? I felt that I had lived an eternity in that silent homage to the Sage.

In the afternoon, the Sage takes his meals in the dining hall along with his devotees and visitors. To eat food served with loving hands and kindly eyes in that ethereal silence is not only bodily nourishment but a tonic to the soul.

In the evening, in the broad verandah of the hall facing the West, Vedic hymns are sung and the Sage sits silent like a sphynx, absorbed in deep meditation. In that pindrop silence, the thoughts of God, His Love, His Grace, His Mercy, His Beatitude come surging in our hearts, like the waves of the wide ocean. As the sun goes down behind the fringe of the surrounding hill, amidst the chorus of the redounding hymns sung with celestial lustre in the eyes, the feeling sweeps you, of the One Stupendous WHOLE embracing all in that vibrant touch of Light and Love, Peace and Harmony.

The sage is a treasure house of Peace and Compassion. He wants every one to crush his ego and to rise to that transcendental height to which he has risen by devotion to God. As we sit at the feet of the Master in what better way can we describe him than what one of the devotees has sung in the following lyrical lines:

"Thou bringeth peace to the troubled minds,
And doubts are scattered by Thy Light;
The thinking brain is soothed to sleep;
And Reason kneeleth at Thy Feet.
Oh, carefree be the happy ones,
Who know the Doer of all things;
They let thee steer the craft of life,
While resting at Thy Blessed Feet.
They learn to see Thee shine in all,
In great and lowly, good and bad;
Their lips no longer speak the blame—
For everywhere they see Thy Feet.
Then how can grateful love express
In feeble words the debt it feels
For Light and Freedom, Joy and Peace
Received from Thee — at Thy Feet?
No wealth or glory, gold or fame,
May lure us from the Holy Shrine
Where Love and Wisdom blend and meet
The heart Divine — the Master's Feet."

(Joyce Riche Heddingh)

SRI RAMANA'S TEACHINGS

Extracts from "Talks with Sri Ramana' Maharashi" published by Sri T.N. Venkataraman, Manager President, Sri Ramanasramam, Tiruvaunamalai, S. Indra.

As is the effect so is the cause. As is the tree so is its seed. The whole tree is contained in the seed which later manifests as the tree. The expanded tree must have a substratum which we call *maya*. As a matter of truth there is neither seed nor tree. There is only Being.

The Name permeates the entire universe densely; who can tell to what depths in the nether regions and to what height in the heaven it extends.

The ignorant fools undergo the eighty-four lakhs of species of births, not knowing the essence of things. The Name is immortal. Forms are in-numerable but Name is all that.

The Name itself is form and form itself is Name. There is no distinction between Name and form. God became manifest and assumed Name and form. Hence the Name the Vedas have established. Beware, there is no mantram beyond the Name. Those who say otherwise are ignorant fools. Name is Keshava Himself. This is known only to the loving devotees of the Lord.

The all-pervading nature of the Name can only be understood when one recognises his own 'I'. When one's own name is not recognised, it is impossible to get the all-pervading Name. When one knows oneself then one finds the Name everywhere.

None can realise the Name by the practice of knowledge, meditation or austerity. Surrender yourself at first at the feet of the Guru and learn to know who the 'I' in you is. After finding the source of that 'I' merge your individuality in that oneness —which is Self-existent and devoid of all duality. It is that Name that permeates the three worlds.

The Name is *Paramatman* Itself where there is no action arising out of *dvaita* (duality).

A *jivanmukta* is one who does not see anything separate from the self.

The objective visions have no intrinsic value.

One cannot see God and yet retain individuality. The seer and the seen unite into one Being. There is no cogniser, nor cognition, nor the cognised. All merge into One Supreme Siva only.

Give up thoughts. That is happiness and also meditation.

To bring about peace means to be free from thoughts and to abide as Pure Consciousness. If one remains at peace oneself, there is only peace all about.

The world is only an idea. You see it when you are awake and not when asleep.

There is no creation in the state of realisation. When one sees the world, one does not see oneself. When one sees the self, the world is not seen. So see the self and realise that there has been no creation.

Saints are the saviours and liberators.

Happiness is not to be sought in solitude or in busy centres. It is in the Self.

The *jnani* acts unawares. Others see him act, but he does not know it himself.

What is *maya?* The knowledge that the mind is divorced from the Reality is *maya*. The mind is in Reality only and not apart.

Be still and know that I AM GOD.

Time and space are functions of thoughts. If thoughts do not arise there will be no future or the Earth.

No one is away from the Self. So each one is Self-realised. Yet, what a mystery that no one knows this fundamental fact, and desires to realise the Self? This ignorance is due to the mistaking of the body for the Self. Realisation now consists in getting rid of this false idea that one is not realised. Realisation is not anything newly got. It must be already there in order that it may be permanent. Otherwise Realisation is not worth attempting.

After the false notion 'I-am-the-body' or 'I have not realised' is removed, Supreme Consciousness or the Self alone is left over, which is however called Realisation in the present state of knowledge. However, the truth is that Realisation is eternal and already there, here and now.

Finally, Realisation amounts to elimination of ignorance and nothing more or less.

Until realisation there will be *karma*, i.e., action and reaction. After realisation there will be no *karma*, no world.

Misery is due to objects. If they are not there, there will be no contingent thoughts and so misery is wiped off. The Self is the only Reality which permeates and also envelops the world.

Dhyana, bhakti, japa, etc., are aids to keep out the multiplicity of thoughts.

Birth and death are only ideas.

"I-am-the-body" idea will become extinct only on Self-Realisation.

So long as there is a subject and also an object it is only relative knowledge. *Jnana* lies beyond relative knowledge. It is absolute.

Reality lies beyond subject and object.

The intellect itself realises after continuous practice that it is enabled by some Higher Power to function. It cannot itself reach that Power. So it ceases to function after a certain stage. When it thus ceases to function the Supreme Power is still left there all alone. That is Realisation; that is the finality; that is the goal.

It is thus plain that the purpose of the intellect is to realise its own dependence upon the Higher Power and its inability to reach the same. So it must annihilate itself before the goal is gained.

The only permanent thing is Reality; and that is the Self. You say "I am" , "I am going", "I am speaking", "I am working", etc. Hyphenate "I am" in all of them. Thus I — AM. That is the abiding and fundamental Reality. This truth was taught by God to Moses: "I AM that I — AM". "Be still and know that I — AM God." So "I — AM" is God.

A *jnani* ceases to be a doer. A *jnani* has his *karana sarira* destroyed; the *sthula sarira* (gross body) has no effect on him and is for all practical purposes destroyed too. The *sukshma sarira* (subtle body) alone remains. It is otherwise called *dtivahika sarira*. It is this which is held by all persons after the physical body is given up. And with this they traverse the other *lokas* until another suitable physical body is taken. The *jnani* is supposed to move in *Brahmaloka* with his *sukshma sarira*. Then that is also dissolved and he passes to final Liberation.

The *Brahman* is no other than the *jnani's* mind.

The Highest Form of Grace is Silence. It is also the highest *upadesa*.

First surrender and see.

Craving for pleasures should not be encouraged. One cannot put out burning fire by pouring petrol over it.

Thoughts form your bondage.

God's name is effective.

Desire constitutes *maya* and Desirelessness is God.

Mauna is the utmost eloquence. Peace is utmost activity.

Pleasure and pain are the aspects of the mind only.

Pain or pleasure is the result of past *karma* and not of the present *karma*.

Liberation is not anywhere outside of you. It is only within. If a man is anxious for Deliverance, the Guru within pulls him in and the Guru without pushes him into the Self. This is the Grace of the Guru.

Heart-talk is all talk. All talk must end in silence only.

A man's true name is *mukti* (liberation).

Let us know our Self and then enquire concerning the Creator and creation. Without first knowing the Self, to seek knowledge of God, etc., is ignorance.

A man can live happily only if he knows that he requires nothing wherewith to live.

When we see our Self there is no world, and when we lose sight of the Self we get ourselves bound in the world.

Surrender consists in giving up oneself and one's possessions to the Lord of Mercy. Then what is left over for the man? Nothing — neither himself nor his possessions. The body liable to be born and to die having been made over to the Lord, the man need no longer worry himself about it. Then birth and death cannot strike terror. The cause of fear was the body; it is no longer his, why should he fear now? Or where is the identity of the individual to be frightened?

Thus the Self is realised and Bliss results. This is then the subject-matter: freedom from misery and gain of Happiness. This is the highest good to be gained. Surrender is synonymous with Bliss itself. This is the relationship.

The ego, the world and the creator are the fundamentals underlying the illusion. If they are known to be not apart from the Self there will be no more illusion.

Silence is the Highest of all achievements.

If you are firm in your belief in the guidance of God, stick to it, and do not concern yourself with what happens around you. Furthermore, there may be happiness or misery. Be equally indifferent to both and abide in the faith of God. That will be so only when one's faith is strong that God looks after all of us.

The Self is the most intimate and eternal Being whereas the *siddhis* are foreign. The one requires effort to acquire and the other does not.

The powers are sought by the mind which must be kept alert, whereas the Self is realised when the mind is destroyed. The powers manifest only when there is the ego. The ego makes you aware of others and in its absence there are no others to be seen. The Self is beyond the ego and is realised after the ego is eliminated. The elimination of the ego makes one un-aware of others. How can the question of others arise and where is the use of occult powers for a Self-Realised Being?

Self-Realisation may be accompanied by occult powers or it may not be. If the person had sought such powers before Realisation, he may get the powers after realisation. There are others who had not sought such powers and had attempted only Self-Realisation. They do not manifest such powers.

These powers may also be sought and gained even after Self-Realisation. But then they are used for a definite purpose, i.e., the benefit of others, as in the case of Chudala.

Unless a person has annihilated his mind he cannot gain peace and be happy. Unless he himself is happy he cannot bestow happiness on others.

Samadhi is one's essential nature.

Your nature is simple Being, free from thoughts.

Find who you are. If you cease to identify yourself with the body no question regarding creation, birth, death, etc., will arise. They did not arise in your sleep. Similarly they will not arise in the true state of the Self.

The object of creation is thus clear, that you should proceed from where you find yourself and realise your true Being.

You could not raise the question in your sleep because there is no creation there. You raise the question now because your thoughts appear and there is creation. Creation is thus found to be only your thoughts.

A person seeks happiness and learns that God alone can make one happy. He prays to God and worships Him. God hears his prayers, and responds by appearing in human shape as a Master in order to speak the language of the devotee and make him understand the Reality. The Master is thus God manifest in human being. He gives out His experience so that the seeker might also gain it. His experience is to abide as the Self. The Self is within.

God, Master and the Self are therefore seeming stages in the Realisation of the Truth.

The Self is pure consciousness and non-dual. It cannot say 'I'. No one says 'I' in sleep. What is the ego then? It is something intermediate between the inert body and the self.

One must be like a child before he advances spiritually, for the ego is not developed in the child.

Intellect is only an instrument of the Self. It cannot help you to know what is beyond itself. The intellect makes you see things outside, and not that which is its own source.

Duality is the characteristic of the ego. When thoughts arise, duality is present; know it to be the ego, and seek its source.

5

DR. ANNIE BESANT

There are few books which stir the human soul to such heights of sublimity as Dr. Mrs. Annie Besant's Autobiography. It is the romance of a noble soul, shunning hypocrisy and cant, courting disasters after disasters and fighting tooth and nail for the vindication of Truth, as conceived from time to time. We see in her a woman of noble aspirations, of purity of thought, of a burning and abiding love for those particularly who are the victims of unjust social laws and customs.

Born of Irish parents, she was brought up in a highly religious environment and was a pet child of both her parents. The first shadow of darkness was cast upon her peaceful home, when her father, the bread-winner of the house died and the mother and the daughter were left alone to fight the grim battle of life in want and penury.

Annie Besant was married much against her will to a clergyman to satisfy the wish of her mother whom she loved the most in life. But the marriage ended in disaster. How could a woman nurtured and nourished in the highest spiritual atmosphere, kept away from the mundane things of life, and fed upon Platonic visions of love, reconcile herself to homely duties of married slavery and pay obedience to a husband who lorded her and disdained her in every respect and whose singularly narrow-minded conception of religion at last drove her to desperation. They were separated and she left her husband's shelter with her tiny babe in her arms, to fight the battle of life alone in the world. Her mother implored her on bended knees, not to leave her husband's home. It was the bitterest and hardest trial to refuse her, whom she loved and adored but she steeled her heart against her entreaties, for she said, that she would not be untrue to her inner self. This is what she writes in her autobiography:

"It seemed like a crime to bring such anguish on her; and I felt like a murderer as the snowy head was pressed against my knees. And yet, — to live a lie? Not even for her was that shame possible in that worst crisis of blinding agony; my will clung fast to Truth. And it is true now and as it ever was, that he who loves father and mother better than Truth is not worthy of her and the flint-strewn path of honesty is the way to Light and Peace."

She preferred to face the cruel world. She had to earn her livelihood, for the pittance which her husband gave her was a cruel mockery. She started her career as a cook and a nurse and eventually with the help of some good friends, she just managed to eke out a living by means of her powerful pen. She joined the Society of Free Thinkers of which Charles Bradlaugh was a conspicuous member. He was a man of most adorable traits of character — loving, kind, sympathetic, humane and most considerate in his behaviour to others. He and Mrs. Besant became thick friends. She found happiness in his company. They both took pride in their anti-religious views. Mrs. Annie Besant became a confirmed atheist. She considered atheism as the highest ethics and took glory in the part she played. Were not Copernicus, Voltaire, Bruno, Spinoza, Priestlay — all atheists? Were they not great souls fired by the burning desire of doing good to humanity; were they not intellectual giants who led a clean and useful life? She considered athesits to be the saviours of the world who faced the damping blows of a merciless world with a heroism worthy of the highest cause. Look at the paneygric which in her unripe wisdom, she showered upon atheists:

"The saviours of the world are too often howled at as atheists and then worshipped as Deities. The atheists are the vanguard of the army of Free Thought on whom falls the brunt of the battle and are shivered the hardest of blows; their feet trample down the thorns that others may tread unwounded; their bodies fill up the ditch that by the bridge thus made, others may pass to victory. Honour to the pioneers of progress, honour to the vanguard of Liberty's army, honour to those who to improve earth have forgotten heaven and who in their zeal for man have forgotten God." (The Gospel of Atheism by Annie Besant.)

It is not for us to raise the finger of disapproval against this noble woman who maddened by the sting of adverse circumstances threw herself headlong into the clouds of doubt and darkness. "What we are concerned is the honesty of her motives, the sincerity of her actions, and above all her love for humanity which prompted her to take action in cleansing the society of its impurities and abscesses. Fearlessness, self-reliance and the eagerness to espouse lost causes, coupled with love for the poor and the downtrodden formed the chief characteristics of this great and noble woman. She endured incredible storms of opposition with the spirit of a martyr. Her heart was fortified with the thought that she was fighting for Truth. Her entire loyalty was to Truth as she conceived it and this landed her into many difficulties and hardships. Her humane heart melted at the sight of want and poverty, disease and sickness. The poor generally beget many children, whom they are not able to maintain and who become either idiots or criminals. It was an economic question.

Dr. Charles Knowlton, a follower of the teachings of Malthus, wrote a pamphlet, urging people to limit their families. It was purely a physiological treatise. It advocated "conjugal prudence" and "parental responsibility." To speak in the words of Mrs. Annie Besant, "Dr. Knowlton advocated the restriction of the number of the family within the means of subsistence and stated the methods by which this restriction could be carried out. The book was never challenged till a discreditable book-seller put some copies for sale to which he added some improper pictures and he was prosecuted and convicted. The publisher of the 'National Reformer' and of Mr. Bradlaugh's and my books and pamphlets among other literature was prosecuted and to our great dismay, he pleaded guilty."

To Mrs. Besant, the conviction of the publisher was a challenge to muzzle the right of free expression of thought. She therefore undertook to publish the pamphlet herself in a separate press and thus defy the State and volunteered also to sell the copies herself. She knew the implications of the action. She knew that her own unsullied name would be stained by defending the cause of a book, which was to all intents and purposes not devoid of obscenity.

She wrote in her autobiography: "I had seen the misery of the poor, of my sister women with children crying for bread, the wages of the workmen were often sufficient for four, but eight or ten they could not maintain. Should I set my own safety, my own good name, against the helping of these? Did it matter that my reputation should be ruined, if its ruin helped to bring remedy to this otherwise helpless wretchedness of thousands? What was worth all my talk about sacrifice and self surrender, if brought to the test, I failed? So, with heart aching, but steady, I came to my resolution, and though I know now that I was wrong intellectually and blundered in the remedy, I was right morally in the will to sacrifice all to help the poor and I can rejoice that I faced a storm of obloquy fiercer and harder to bear than any other which can ever touch me again." (Mrs. Annie Besant's Autobiography, page 208).

Mrs. Besant was tried, convicted and then let go. But the worst calamity followed. The cruel husband brought upon her a charge that her Atheism and Malthusianism made her unfit to be the guardian of her daughter. The court gave a verdict in favour of her husband and the mother was deprived of her precious treasure — her own child. It was a severe blow. It broke her health and she fell dangerously ill but she eventually recovered from her long illness.

Her struggle and sacrifice were however not without reward. The Law afterwards removed the stigma on marriage by enacting that not the husband but the wife had claim on their issues.

Deprivation of her daughter was a hard pill for Mrs. Besant to swallow but she carried on her lonely journey through life with a resolute will. She became a mother to the orphaned children of the world. She took up also the cause of Socialism and worked day and night. It brought about a schism between her and her most devoted friend and ally — Charles Bradlaugh: She gave up the joint editorship of Bradlaugh's "The National Reformer" with the view that he may not be embarrassed. It was a great trial, but she was a woman, whose loyalty to Truth was so great that she never hesitated to bear any amount of suffering for the sake of truth as she conceived it.

We have seen Mrs. Besant so far as engaged in the struggles of life, with her mind endued with the materialistic conception of things. But she was soon to go through a transformation. She came in contact with W.T. Stead, the editor of the *Pall Mall Gazette*, and they became thick friends — he a Christian and she an Atheist. They both projected the scheme of founding a half-penny weekly, the object of which was to build a New Church dedicated to the service of man. It was at this time that Mrs. Besant began to feel some strange longings, something loftier than she had ever felt before. She took to the study of Spiritualism. She was convinced by her own experiments that the phenomena of Clairvoyance, Clairaudience and thought reading were real. Let us describe the state of her mind, at this stage of her life in her own words.

"I finally convinced myself that there was some hidden thing, some hidden power and resolved to seek until I found and by the early spring of 1889 I had grown desperately determined to find at all hazards what I sought. At last sitting alone in deep thought as I had become accustomed to do after the sun had set, filled with an intense but nearly hopeless longing to solve the riddle of life and mind, I heard a voice that was later to become to me the holiest sound on earth, bidding me take courage for the light was near."

Yes, the light was near. The hidden hands of God, had tried the young votary of Truth in all the diverse ways and found her not wanting. She had been put to hardest tests. Purified and exalted by the spirit of self-lessness and eager desire to perceive and follow nothing else but Truth, she walked through all the labyrinths of life and ultimate by with the grace of God, she landed herself on the sure path of the Divine Self. The voice that she said, she had heard but could not identify clearly was the voice of God — the flicker of the divine light that was soon to dawn on her and lift up the veil of ignorance which had tied her so long to the valley of doubt and darkness.

A fortnight after she had heard the inner voice, Mr. Stead put into her hands two bulky volumes of "The Secret Doctrine" written by Madame Blavatsky.

"Can you review these? My young men all fight shy of them, but you are quite mad enough on these subjects to make something of them."

The secret door of her heart was opening. She took the books reverently and brought them home to devour them with extreme delight and gusto. This is what she writes in her autobiography:

"As I turned over page after page the interest became absorbing; but how familiar it seemed; how my mind leapt forward to presage the conclusions, how natural it was, how coherent, how subtle and yet how intelligible. I was dazzled, blinded by the light in which disjointed facts were seen as parts of a mighty whole and all my puzzles, riddles, problems, seemed to disappear. The effect was partially illusive in one sense in that they all had to be slowly unravelled later, the brain gradually assimilating that which the swift intuition had grasped as truth. But the light had been seen and in the flash of illumination I knew that the weary search was over and the very Truth was found."

Mrs. Besant reviewed the books and that brought her into intimate association with Madame Blavatsky, the founder of the world wide Theosophical Society. She soon became a Theosophist. The materialist became a mystic. The woman who was restless in her struggles, soon now realized as her soul was illumined the blessings of a tranquil mind. But it was not without a great wrench of heart that she joined the Theosophical Society. Through out her chequered career, she had experienced great sufferings, all for truth as she conceived, at the time and now when she was on the threshold of the Real Truth, she had again to face great difficulties, the worst of which was the separation from the life long companionship of such a great and lofty-minded man, as Charles Bradlaugh. It was not only Bradlaugh, but other innumerable friends, who had fought shoulder to shoulder with her in many battles of life, for the vindication of social rights and justice and whom she would now miss. But she was resolute. She was willing to give up everything. Her inner eyes were now opened and with the knowledge of God and the secrets of nature, even the most sacred friendships mattered little to her.

Mrs. Besant's friendship with Madame Blavatsky was the happiest chapter in her life. When Madame Blavatsky was attacked and maligned in the press as a result of a mean conspiracy of her maid servant and her husband — the notorious Coulombs and when the Psychic Research Society issued a false report against this Russian sage and mystic, it was Mrs. Annie Besant who took up cudgel on behalf of Madame Blavatsky and exposed the conspirators. Hers was a most spirited defence based on facts and commonsense.

With Mrs. Besant's joining the Theosophical movement the field of service became much larger for her and she immersed herself headlong into varied activities. Being a fluent speaker and wielding a powerful pen she was able by means of her oratory and writing to considerably augment the vista of the Theosophical Movement. Her talents were employed for the furtherance of the Theosophic cause through out the world. She was the President of the Society for a number of years. She founded the Hindu Benares University in India. She took a most prominent part in Indian politics and helped the progress of India on all sides — political, educational, moral, social, and religious.

The record of Mrs. Besant's service is unique. The vast number of books written on Theosophy and religion particularly is an index of her industry and tireless devotion. We give below a few of her works, which are a landmark in the literature of spiritual philosophy and which reveal the growth and development of a soul highly sensitive to sublimity of thought and full of intuitive illumination: *The Ancient Wisdom, Brahmavidya, Dharma, Esoteric Christianity, Hints on the Study of Bhagvad Gita, In the Outer Court, An Introduction to Yoga, Mysticism, The Path of Discipleship, A Study in Consciousness, The Wisdom of the Upanishads, The Masters, The Four Religions* (Christianity, Hinduism, Zoroastrianism, Islam).

Dr. Mrs. Besant was one of the first to translate into English from Sanskrit the *Bhagvad Gita* and in order to popularise it, she got the book printed and sold at a very nominal cost of four annas. The Bhagvad Gita is the most mystical book in the world and her services in broadcasting the tenets and teachings of the Gita should be ever remembered with loving gratitude. Her belief in the Masters and her contacts with these Elder Brothers, as she fondly calls them, constitute a rich chapter in the life history of this great and noble woman. Though the world may still hesitate and jest at the thought of supernormal agencies working in the universe for the good of all mankind, it will not be denied that slowly and steadily it will veer round to the teaching of the Theosophists, who have done wonderful work in lifting the veil. *The Voice of the Silence, At the Feet of the Master* and *The Light on the*

Path are gems in the literature of Mysticism of the world and the exhaustive commentaries made by Dr. Besant in collaboration with Bishop Leadbeater form a distinct contribution of invaluable nature to the occult knowledge of the world, in modern times.

With characteristic energy and devotion Mrs. Besant made a deep comparative study of all the religions of the world and her effort in establishing the unity and synthesis as existing in the fundamental teachings of all the religions is a contribution of no mean order. This unity of thought, this non-separateness is the basic idea in the teaching of mysticism and in establishing the brotherhood of men on the foundation rock of divine unity in diversity of forms, Dr. Besant has only added her contribution to the storehouse of Indian spirituality. Though an Englishwoman, she was so much touched by the lofty idealism contained in the Hindu scriptures, that she discarded her Western dress and put on a sari. Western in body, she was Eastern in soul and she worked like a Trojan, sacrificing herself in every respect for the good of India and the world.

The debt which this country owes to this singularly unselfish and heroic woman, it will be hard to repay. An extremely strong advocate of Truth, she was loyal to it, throughout the chequered career of her life. She never wavered, she never hesitated to immolate herself, when duty demanded such a sacrifice. She used to say and it was true that she never purchased peace with a lie. She always spoke the truth and acted truth. "That one loyalty to Truth. I must keep stainless, whatever friendships fail me or human ties be broken. She may lead me into the wilderness, yet I must follow her; she may strip me of all love, yet I must pursue her, though she slay me, yet will I trust in her; and ask no other epitaph on my tomb but

"She tried to follow Truth."

The Theosophists have their motto, "There is no religion, greater than Truth." Dr. Besant lived Truth. She was the highest embodiment of Truth and Truth is God.

6

SRI RAMA KRISHNA

India is a land of saints and seers. What has sustained this great continent in its chequered career is the spirituality of its ancient culture and civilisation. *The Bhagvad Gita* and the *Upanishads*, the heritage of the distant past, remind us that with the people of India, religion is an instinct and not a dead force. Spiritual India, it is said may become one day the saviour of the whole world. India's spirituality is her greatest contribution to the culture and civilisation of the world. The deep-rooted strength of her religious tradition can be gauged from the fact, that inspite of vicissitudes of time she has not failed to produce spiritual giants capable of transforming the whole world.

One of such highly evolved spiritual personages was Sri Rama Krishna Paramahamsa who was born in Bengal in 1836. He may be taken as the embodiment of the spirit of India's culture and religion. His biographer Romain Rolland, the great French savant has made the name and teaching of Sri Rama Krishna, famous throughout the world. In fact, the Rama Krishna Mission founded after the death of this great mystic, is now a world-wide institution, with its branches spread not only in India, but in America and different countries of Europe.

Rama Krishna even in his childhood and boyhood showed extraordinary mental and spiritual tendencies. When he was hardly six or seven years old, it is said, walking along a narrow path, through the rice fields, looking upon the sky, he saw a beautiful thunder-cloud and as it gradually covered the whole sky, a flock of birds flew overhead. The beauty of the phenomenon made a deep and abiding impression upon the young boy. He went into raptures and fell down in ecstasy. He was picked up in an unconscious state of mind. Often, while playing in a village dramatic performance, he would go into a deep trance. Trances and ecstasies became a part of Rama Krishna's life, right from the early age.

Such a boy could hardly be fit for ordinary education and training. He was a failure at the school. In fact, he avoided schooling. His apathy to school education was so great, that when he was admonished, he would say, "Brother, what shall I do with a mere bread-winning education. I would rather acquire that wisdom which would illumine my heart and getting which one is satisfied for ever." The boy's hunger was for spiritual attainments that could give him eternal satisfaction. His love for solitude and indifference to worldy affairs, became more and more pronounced and he felt extremely happy when he was put in charge of the image of the Mother Kali, in the temple on the bank of the Ganges at Dakshineswar.

But his religious fervour was so great that he proved a hopeless failure in carrying out the routine duties of a Brahmin priest. He would sit and stare at the goddess for hours together and fall in meditation. His hunger to get a vision of the Mother so overpowered him that people looked upon him as a mad man, who had no control over his mind and acted in a very stupid manner. Only a few understood his spiritual intoxication and they looked upon him with admiration and adoration.

Rama Krishna gives an account of his first spiritual experience in the following lines.

"I was then suffering from excruciating pain because I had not been blessed with the vision of the mother. I felt as if my heart were being squeezed like a wet towel. I was overpowered by a great restlessness and a fear that it might not be my lot to realize Her in this life. I could not bear the separation any longer, life did not seem worth living. Suddenly my eyes fell on the sword that was kept in the Mother's temple. Determined to put an end to my life I jumped up like a madman and seized it, when suddenly the blessed Mother revealed Herself to me and I fell unconscious on the floor. What exactly happened after that, or how that day or the next day passed, I do not know, but within me there was a steady flow of undiluted bliss altogether new and I felt the presence of the Divine Mother."

Having once gained the vision of the Divine Mother, Rama Krishna's anxiety for such repeated visions became more marked. He constantly prayed for it and he bitterly cried, when he did not succeed. He never felt abashed when people gathered round him. To him they were like shadows or painted pictures. His whole heart, mind and soul were as if it were absorbed in the thought of the Kali Mata and he suffered excruciating pain at the thought of separation. Eventually, when he began to get visions systematically, his attitude changed. He was then like a child, submissive to the will of the Mother. He would say, "O Mother, I have taken refuge in Thee, teach me, what to do or say. Thy will is paramount everywhere and is for the benefit of Thy children. Merge my ego in Thy will and make me Thy instrument."

Such is the outburst of heart, in fact, of all mystics. The mystics never ask for any favour for themselves. They always pray that they may be made the instruments of God to carry out His design of evolution.

As years grew, Shri Rama Krishna's visions became a common affair. He could call for them at His will. But he had to pay a heavy price for it. He suffered bodily tortures. His skin was on fire. No earthly physician could cure his ailment, which was purely spiritual. Inwardly he was at rest, but he suffered from sleeplessness and his body was a furnace of fire. Let us describe his further experiences, in his own words:

"No sooner was one stage transcended than another took its place. Before the whirlwind the sacred thread was blown away. Not only that, even the wearing cloth hardly remained. The idea of caste lost all meaning for me. A low caste man sent me his curry cooked, by his wife which I ate with relish. In the Panchavati I would sit in deep meditation with my body perfectly still — losing all consciousness of the outside world. At that time for want of proper care, my hair was matted. Birds would perch on my head and peck the grains of rice left there during the time of worship. Often snakes would crawl over my motionless body and neither I nor the snakes knew it. O, what visions flitted past my eyes, day and night!

"As I sat down to meditate, I would find a *Sanyasin* emerging from my body, trident in hand, directing me to concentrate my mind on God, leaving aside all other thoughts, He threatened to plunge his weapon into my body if I did not do so — The ordinary man could not bear a fraction of the tremendous fervour: his body would be shattered by a quarter of that emotion, I could forget my indescribable pangs only by seeing the Mother in some form or the other for the greater part of the day and night. I could not close the eyelids however much I might try to do so.

"I had no idea of time nor of the body. When the mind at rare intervals came down to a lower plane and I had a faint idea of the body, a shudder of pain would pass through me at the thought that

I was going mad. Standing before a mirror I would put my finger into my eyes to see if the eyelids would close, but they would not. Horrified, I would often burst into tears and pray, 'Mother is this the result of praying and wholly surrendering myself unto Thee? Ah, Thou hast visited me with a fell disease. But the next moment I would say, 'Let it be as Thou wisheth. Let this body go to pieces, but leave me not. Reveal Thyself to me, be kind to Thy helpless son, O Mother, I have taken shelter at Thy lotus feet, Thou art my only refuge! As I prayed thus, my mind would again be stimulated, this body would seem a trifle, not worth thinking about and the blissful Mother would appear before me and console me with Her gracious words."

A Brahamini came into contact with Sri Rama Krishna and recognising the spiritual nature of his bodily suffering, she administered to him a yogic treatment which at once made him whole and his pain disappeared. The treatment consisted of wearing a garland of fragrant flowers and painting his body with sandal paste. The Brahamini was a highly evolved woman and a perfected soul.

It was this Brahamini, who declared that Sri Rama Krishna was an incarnation of God and to prove the bona fides of her statement, she invited scholars and saints to see Rama Krishna. They came and they were satisfied.

The Brahamini, we are told acted as his spiritual guide for some time. She initiated him into the secrets of the Tantric practices. In fact, he became an expert in all kinds of devotional practices, and attained to what is called *Nirvikalpa Samadhi.* —"the highest flight of Advaita philosophy." People generally laugh at and ridicule the practices of the mystics and consider their contacts with the Absolute as fantastic and chimerical. This kind of attitude to undermine the claim of the mystics is wrong. Evelyn Underhill says in her beautiful book, *Mysticism, A Study in the Nature and Development of Man's Spiritual Consciousness:* "Mystics are the pioneers of the spiritual world and we have no right to deny validity to their discoveries, merely because we lack the opportunity or the courage necessary to those who would prosecute such explorations for themselves." (Page 4)

To understand spiritual giants like Sri Rama Krishna and others, we have to discard certain prejudices and entirely change our mental conceptions. As Evelyn Underhill says, "We must pull down our own card houses" and get into the strain of the mystic's mind. The mystic considers the visible world as nothing and by a severe type of renunciation he is able to rend the veil, which hides the "Isis" and come to the Reality — the Absolute Truth.

Sri Rama Krishna's longing for the Absolute was so strong, that it was entirely due to his persistent efforts, his great piety and austerity, that he succeeded in lifting the curtain and seeing God face to face.

The great beauty of Sri Rama Krishna's religious experiences is that he employed the different methods and means of various religions to realize God. He was initiated in the truths of the Vedanta philosophy and religion by a monk called Totapuri. Holy mantras were chanted and the pupil carried out all the instructions of the *guru,* renouncing, "all desire for enjoyment here and hereafter." Totapuri had taken forty long years to realize the Absolute Spirit in the true Vedantic fashion but to his great surprise he saw that Sri Rama Krishna realized God in the space of mere three days. What a tremendous contrast!

When Rama Krishna attained *Nirvikalpa Samadhi* he tried to realize God by the methods of other faiths, viz., Islam and Christianity and he succeeded marvelously. His biographer says, "This as a result of his realization through all forms of discipline, he was firmly convinced that all religions were true, that every doctrinal system represented a path to God. The three great systems of thought, known as Dualism, Qualified Monism and Monism — Dvaita, Vishtadvaita and Advaita — he perceived to be but different stages in man's progress towards the goal. He held that they were not contradictory but complimentary being suited to different mental outlooks."

Though Rama Krishna did not like that any reference should be made to his being an Incarnation of God, he did look upon himself as such, having realised God, through the channels of various religions, which he characterized as different paths, leading to the same object — God. This is what he said to his disciples regarding his various religious experiences.

"I have practised all religions, — Hinduism, Islam, Christianity and I have also followed the paths of the different Hindu sects. I have found it is the same God towards. Whom all are directing their steps, though along different paths."

"The tank has several ghats. At one Hindus draw water in pitchers and call it *jal:* at another Mohammadans draw water in leathern bottles and call it *pani:* at a third Christians draw water and they call it water. Can we imagine that the water is not *jal,* but only pani or water? How absurd! The substance is one under different names and every one is seeking the same substance.

"Every religion of the world is one such ghat. Go direct with a sincere and earnest heart by any of these ghats and you will reach the water of Eternal Bliss. But say not that your religion is better than that of another."

It is said in the Christian Bible, "You are predestined to act as a Spirit in touch with God here and now, but God does not force you to undertake this responsibility, yet He urges you to do for your own sake."

Yes, God urges us to realize Him for our own sake, for our own happiness but we are so foolish that we succumb to the devastating pleasures of the senses. We do not care for the substance but run after the mere shadow and form. Lives of such great souls, as Sri Rama Krishna are like beacon lights to show us the way. Every one of us can realize God, in this very life. What is wanted is resoluteness of purpose, lofty idealism, persistence of effort and knowledge. The Bible says, "You are stronger than the flesh, more powerful than earthly fate, for your destiny is to be a son or daughter of the King of Kings and your Home is in God's Land."

Such glorious is the destiny of man namely to become one of the Family of God, to be united with Him. And what can bring this achievement? Says Ramkrishna, 'I and Mine' is ignorance. 'Thou and Thine' is knowledge. We can become free when we divest ourselves of all thoughts of self and egotism and practise spiritual exercises in the spirit of absolute obedience to the will of God. It is God's will that we should all see Him. It is not a distant goal. It is not an impractical proposition. Saints and mystics have seen God with and without form.

Says Rama Krishna "As wet wood put on a furnace loses its moisture gradually, so the moisture of worldliness dies away of itself from the man who has taken refuge in God and the repeats His holy name. He who intends to think of God, after his attachment to things has ceased will never be able to do so for that time will never come."

It is true the worldly mingled never come to their senses. Shri Rama Krishna compares them to camels, who are fond of thorny shrubs. "The more they eat of them, the more their mouths bleed yet they do not refrain from making them their food."

Saints and seers like Rama Krishna and others are like beautiful flowers emanating light and fragrance, which we all need in the sandy desert of our journey. We are all mediums. In each one of us there is the spark of divinity. It is for every one of us to realize the latent force in this spark and become a god.

Rama Krishna was married to Sarada Devi a girl barely fourteen years old. He allowed her the privilege to reign as queen in his house hold, but he did not allow her to entertain any mundane ideas. He spiritualised her and looked upon her as Divine Mother. Their relationship with each other was not of husband and wife and not even, when they lived to gather did any sensuous thought ever cross their minds. Rama Krishna was an incarnation of God in the eyes of the young girl, who adored him as such and paid her reverent homage to her divine Lord and Rama Krishna likewise looked upon her as divine Mother. Both their minds were attuned to God.

Of all the monastic disciples of Sri Rama Krishna, Swami Vivekananda, known in his earlier years, as Narenda Nath Dutt was the most favourite. When Rama Krishna died of cancer of the throat in 1886, Swami Vivekananda paid the following most glowing tribute to his *guru*:

"The books are theories, he was the realization. This man had in fifty one years lived the five thousand years of national spiritual life and so raised himself to be an object lesson for future generations."

7

MAHATMA GANDHI

There is no greater figure today in the history of the world than that of Mahatma Gandhi, — the apostle of truth and non-violence. He is the soul of spiritual India, — a mystic whose vision transcends the mundane and whose actions are dictated or influenced by the soul's inner voice.

Gandhiji resembles Count Leo Tolstoy in many ways. Like him when he was young, he took to a gay life. When he went to England to appear for the Bar, the young lad, — Mohandas Karamchand Gandhi, in spite of his promises to his mother that he would keep away from pleasures, entered headlong into the snare of *maya*. When he returned from England, none knew that this Indian barrister finely dressed in English costume, with English manners and tastes, would soon discard the finery of English civilisation and education and become a half-naked fakir, working for the political and spiritual emancipation of his country.

The transformation of Gandhiji from a fop into a fakir reminds us of Count Leo Tolstoy. In his young age, Tolstoy was a worshipper of the pleasures of the senses. He sucked every drop of the so called pleasure and at last got so sick of it that he discarded the cloth of empty tinsel and broke to pieces the cup of poison which he had drunk too long. He became a reformed man. The sorrows and sufferings of the poor made a home in his heart. He became the champion of the oppressed and the suppressed. He renounced the luxuries, to which he was accustomed as a count, and led the life of an ordinary man, cobbling his own shoes and working on the farm tending his cattle and ploughing the fields. He was instrumental in laying the foundation stone of a free Russia, when the revolution of 1917 ushered into quite a new era in the history of that country — an era of freedom and social justice.

What Tolstoy did in Russia, Gandhijee did in India, with this difference that India's liberation is the immediate result of Gandhijee's sacrifices, Tolstoy was only a fore-runner and not an actual participant in the great Soviet Revolution.

It was South Africa which gave a new birth to Gandhiji. It changed the whole course of his life. Hardly had he landed on the soil of India, after his return from England, than he was engaged by an Indian firm, as a barrister to fight their case in South Africa. When he was travelling from Durban to Pretoria, he had a first class ticket, but at an intermediate station he was stopped, for he had not purchased any ticket for bedding and he was turned out from his compartment by an unruly guard. It hurt him but it opened his inward eye. He passed a whole night in a dark waiting room ruminating in his mind upon the incident of the day and the harshness of the treatment meted out to him. The gross injustice done to him kindled his soul. He began to think of the hard lot of his own Indian brothers in the country. He at once decided that he should sacrifice his life. The man who came to earn money for himself at once embarked upon a new venture. He became a *satayagrahi.* He launched his movement of non-violence — satyagraha — against the iniquities heaped upon his Indian brothers in South Africa. And he succeeded marvelously well. That bitter night which he had spent alone in the waiting-room, slapped and kicked by an unruly world, had pierced its fangs in his heart and had made a new man of him. It had awakened his inner conciense, which was lying dormant. That bitter night completely transformed him.

This is what he wrote later on in *Young India* (25th August 1927): "Mankind is notoriously too dense to read the signs that God sends from time to time. We require drums to be beaten into our ears, before we should wake from our trance and hear the warning and see that to lose oneself in all is the only way to find oneself."

Evelyn Underhill in her book, *Mysticism,* says: "In idealism we have perhaps the most sublime theory of Being which has been constructed by the human intellect, a theory so sublime in fact that it can hardly have been produced by the exercise of "pure-reason" alone but must be looked upon as a manifestation of that natural mysticism, that instinct for the Absolute, which is latent in man."

There is divinity hidden in every human soul. It is too true what is said, "I live, yet not I, but God in me." Every one is a child of God. Religion has been man's chief support in life. But unfortunately all the religions have remained so static and there is so much of formalism in them that it is no wonder that they have ceased to exert that beneficent influence which they are supposed to have upon man's character. What man wants is experience and not any formalism that is hedged and hemmed in with creeds and dogmas. Herein then comes the mystic, who understands his relationship with God, who realizes the transcendental virtue of his soul within him and who by earnest longing at last awakens himself to God consciousness.

It is not by reasoning or logic that inward consciousness can be realized. Why is it that Gandhiji is able to come up to the pattern of higher idealism? He is not an orator, a politician, a scientist, a thinker, an inventor, a poet or a learned man. He is quite a simple man, without any claim to brilliancy of intellect. How could such a man wield such a tremendous power on the people? The secret of his success is that he is a man of heart, a man of idealism. Is it not said in the Bible, "The pure in heart shall see God."

If an intellectual man aims at realizing the Reality merely by means of his intellect, his system must break down. It is the mystic alone who "builds the ladder to the stars." For, according to him, the soul is seated in the heart and not in the head. It is the piercing vision of the heart that can realize God and attain to supernatural powers and not cold logic or reasoning which are mere faltering steps, groping in the dark.

When we look at Gandhiji, — that slim, toothless man, hardly weighing seventy pounds of flesh and bones, uncouth in appearance, but for the eyes which shine like stars, we become aware that it is a personality, that does not deserve more than passing notice.

But Gandhiji is a king of mystics. The very fact that he has been able to crush his individuality and has no personality is the sign of his spiritual greatness. He has crushed his "self" to live for universal Self. When he offers his prayers, he always makes himself believe that he is absolutely nothing. His humility and complete absence of egotism are the hall marks of his character. Gandhiji is not a mystic of the type of Sri Rama Krishna Paramahamsa. He does not go into ecstasies. Trances and ecstasies are beyond him. He is a Karma Yogi, to whom work is the breath of his life. He combines strenuous work with devotion to God. But whatever he does, it has first the acceptance of his inner voice. It may appear strange how a man of his temperament could have taken to politics. But it must be remembered that he has spiritual politics.

"Whatever striking things I have done in life. I have not done prompted by reason but prompted by instinct — I would say God." This is what Gandhiji would tell his friends and admirers. He is so much immersed in the thought and love of God, that he would say, "Blast my belief in God and I am dead." Gandhiji's greatest weapon is prayer.

When the Dandi Salt March of 1930 was inaugurated, Gandhiji had no conception what turn it would take. He never reasoned out. He got the idea in a flash and to him it was a divine command, which nothing on the earth could check or stop. His friends, like Pandit Motilal and others tried to dissuade him from taking such a mad course. But he was adamant. He resisted all friendly advice and started on his mad venture. We know how the movement stirred the whole country. The Salt Tax was the most obnoxious tax in the eyes of the people and his open revolt against it created a great furore and fervour among the people. Thousands followed him and the Dandi Salt March was a huge success.

When he announced his various decisions for fasting, they were also the result of the inner voice. Whether he had prophetic vision or not, it is undeniable that his inner voice always prevailed. His faith in God stood him ever in goodstead even in the darkest hour of his trial. In all the storms and struggles of life, he never lost the equanimity of his mind. He maintained a serene and calm attitude, — the coolness of a born sage, in his whole career. On analysis, it would be found that Gandhiji was entirely swayed in all his thoughts and movements by the inner forces working within him. This is what he wrote in one of the issue of "Young India". "I want to identify myself with everything that lives in the language of the Gita. For me there is no politics devoid of religion."

We see in Gandhiji, a peacemaker, a lover of humanity, a worshipper of the Ideal, a keen advocate of the rights of men, a fighter of just causes, a rebel in the sense that he espouses the cause of the suppressed and the depressed. But what strikes us the most in him is his sublime attitude of devotion to God. Some of his best expressions of thought and emotion are to be found in his articles on God and "Prayers" and it would not be amiss to quote a few of the extracts:

"There is nothing that wastes the body like worry and one who has any faith in God should be ashamed to worry about anything whatsoever. It is a difficult rule no doubt for the simple reason that faith in God with the majority of mankind is either an intellectual belief or a blind belief a kind of superstitious fear of something indefinable. But to ensure absolute freedom from worry requires a living utter faith which is a plant of slow, almost unperceived growth and requires to be watered by tears that accompany genuine prayer. They are the tears of a lover who can not brook a moment's separation from the loved one or of the patient who knows that it is some trace of impurity in him that keeps him away from the loved one."

"There is one indefinable Mysterious Power that pervades everything. I feel it though I do not see it."

"I trust men only because I trust God."

"I claim to be a man of faith and prayer and even if I was cut to pieces, God would give me strength not to deny Him and to assert that He is."

"Everyone has faith in God though everyone does not know it. For everyone has faith in himself and that multiplied to the 'n'th degree is God. We may not be God, but we are of God even as a little drop of water is of the ocean. Imagine it torn away from the ocean and flung millions of miles away. It becomes helpless, torn from its surroundings and can not feel the might and majesty of the ocean. But if some one could point out to it that it is of the ocean, its faith would revire, it would dance with joy and the whole of the might and majesty of the ocean would be reflected in it."

"Truth is God and untruth a denial of Him."

"Search for Truth is search for God."

"Truth is God."

"Reliance upon the sword is wholly inconsistent with reliance upon God."

"God requires the purest sacrifice."

"We may learn each one of us to stand alone. God only is our infallible and eternal guide."

"God's existence cannot be, does not need to be proved. God is. If He is not felt, so much the worse for us. The absence of feeling is a disease which we shall some day throw off *nolens rolens*."

"Prayer is not an asking; it is a longing of the soul."

"Prayer is a result of the realization of our helplessness and our final reliance upon God to the exclusion of all else."

"If prayer does not help, nothing else will."

"I believe prayer is the very soul and essence of religion and therefore prayer must be the very core of the life of man, for, no man can live without religion. There are some who in the egoism of their reasoning declare that they have nothing to do with religion. But it is like a man saying that he breathes but he has no nose."

"He who has experienced the magic of prayer may do without food for days together but not a single moment without prayer. For, without prayer there is no inward peace."

"The man of prayer will be at peace with himself and the whole world, the man who goes about the affairs of the world without a prayerful heart will be miserable and will make the world also miserable. Prayer is the only means of bringing about orderliness and peace and repose in our daily acts."

"Prayer has been the saving of my life. Without if I would have been a lunatic long ago."

"The existence of God is like a geometrical axiom."

"If I exist, God exists."

"Our prayer is a heart search. It is a reminder to ourselves that we are helpless without God's support."

"Prayer is a call to humanity. It is a call to self-purification, to inward search."

One of the favourite prayers of Mahatma Gandhi is the following hymn.

> "Lead kindly Light, amid the encircling gloom Lead Thou me on.
>
> The night is dark and I am far from home, Lead Thou me on.
>
> Keep thou my feet, I do not ask to see
>
> The distant scene, one step enough for me
>
> I was not ever thus, nor prayed that thou shouldst lead me on;
>
> I loved to choose and see my path; but now lead Thou me on.
>
> I loved the garrish day, and spite of fears
>
> Pride ruled my will; remember not past years.
>
> So long Thy power hath bleseth me, sure it still Will lead me on.
>
> O'er moor and fen, o'er crag and tor-rent, till the night is gone.
>
> And with the morn those angel faces smile.
>
> Which I have loved long since and lost a while."

A mystic is one who believes in unity of life and in Mahatma Gandhi, we notice this as forming the source and bulwark of all his actions. To him the whole humanity is a Brotherhood and any injury done to any part of it, injures his ownself. Being endowed with imagination of the highest type, it cuts him to pieces at the very thought of violence perpetrated upon any section of the body politic.

The fact that he recently went on foot from village to village both in the Behar and the East Bengal areas, where Hindu-Muslim tension had created a havoc of human lives, preaching to Hindus to resist from their mad fury and imploring his Muslim brothers to think of all, as knit into one band of humanity, shows us Mahatma Gandhi at his best. Mysticism means love of God and love of God means love of all men, without distinction of colour, caste or creed. We cannot have a nobler specimen of humanity than in Gandhiji, to whom toil is the breath of his nostril, to whom suffering and sacrifice are a necessity for the sublimation of his soul, to whom love for all is the crown of his life.

While reading extracts from the Koran in a Hindu temple, before an audience composed for the most part of Hindus, at one of the prayer meetings, he was told by some of them to desist from reading the Koran. His silent rebuke to them was that he would stop the prayers, if he was not allowed to read from the Koran. The prayer meeting dispersed, but the next day the audience understood and realized the significance of Mahatmaji's silent rebuke and the prayers were continued with readings from the Koran.

As a torch bearer of the unity of life, it is difficult in the present age of turmoil and bitter communal strife in India to find an equal to Mahatma Gandhi in liberalism of thought and action.

The poem "Karma Yogi" composed by Sister Lalita applies to Mahatma Gandhi in such a fitting manner, that it is worth quoting it here in extenso:

"Sage and worker
What are you thinking of
What are you seeking
Amid the world's strife?
Not for you the heaven of silence
Not for you the wild forest's peace.

Noise and dust
Of a town's busy traffic,
Hoot of car,
And clatter of feet

People about you
For ever are seeking
Helping or comfort
By word or by deed.

All the demands
Of life made upon you
Facing the struggle
Against odds with a smile.

You too stand lonely

Though crowds press around you
You come from your hill top
To mingle with men.

Courage and faith
In an ultimate purpose
Patience and strength
That keeps you divine.

Light in a city
A guide light to many,
Man living life
For God to shine through."

8

SADHU SUNDERSINGH

When we contemplate upon the life of Sadhu Sundersingh, who was born in Hindu parents, but who became a Christian at the early age of fifteen, as a result of his having seen in a vision the picture of Jesus Christ showering His blessings upon him, we get a glimpse of a truly saintly man of mystical temperament of a high order. He resembles St. Francis of Assissi in many ways, particularly in his love of Christ and all beings sentient and insentient directness of spiritual perception.

Born of Hindu parents in 1889, at Rampur, in the Patiala State, he was baptized in 1905. Even when he was a boy he had great longings and cravings for transcendental wisdom. His heart was hungry for spiritual food and he was thirsting for spiritual water that might quench his thirst for ever. He was not fond of Christianity but one day he fell into a trance and he saw in a vision, Lord Jesus Christ in all His glory. He was carried away by spiritual fervour and rightly or wrongly he gave up his own religion for Christ's sake. He took the vow of poverty and asceticism and went from village to village, clad and clothed in a sadhu's saffron robes, — for being an Indian he metioulously stuck to the Indian garb of the sadhu — and preached to the villagers the simple teachings of Christ, making abundant use of parables, just as his Master did when talking to the poor and the lowly who flocked to hear him.

Sadhu Sundersingh was a man of prayer. He fasted for full forty days after his conversion to get more spiritual insight. It was a miracle how he survived such an ordeal. He had psychic gifts and spiritual powers, especially, spiritual healing, which like Swami Vivekananda, he rarely practised, reserving his energy for the great mission of awakening the spiritual consciousness of the people.

When he went to Tibet to preach Christianity, he was molested and persecuted by the Tibetans, who cast him in a deep well, which was then covered up with a heavy metal lid. Certain death stared at him. The well was full of dirt and dirty smell. But the Sadhu did not feel un-nerved, for he was in communion with high spiritual forces and his life was miraculously saved. At dead of night the lid of the well was removed by some strange invisible hands. A rope was thrown in and he climbed up with the help of that rope, once again, a free man. But he was caught and brought before the tribunal of the Lamas. The latter, when they heard of the miraculous escape of Sundersingh, got so frightened of him, believing him to be a man vested with some magic powers that they let him off immediately. He then went from village to village, spreading the message of Christ, of love and good-will to all and thousands flocked to him to hear him speak of Christ, the Mystic of Mystics, who taught that God lived not in the scriptures but in the human hearts.

Sadhu Sundersingh was a man who radiated joy. "My soul is like an ocean. On the surface there may be waves and tempests but deep down there is undisturbed calm." He was a man of inward peace and was considered as a Christocentric Mystic. His love for Christ was unique; to him partnership with Christ was a sort of a passion, a privilege, which he prized the most. It was for the sake of Christ that he welcomed all sufferings and hardships. They exalted his spirit. The Sadhu's philosophy differed from that of the Hindu ascetic. He did not court sufferings, as our sanyasins do, to get spiritual profit but he welcomed them when inescapable, as a means of service to Christ whom he adored. Religion is a Christ, he would argue in his simple manner. Just as water quenches the physical thirst of man, religion quenches the spiritual thirst of man.

> In which the cordon of the mystery
> In which the heavy and weary weight
> Of all this intelligible world,
> Is lightened that serene and blessed mood
> In which the affections gently lead us on,

Until, the breath of this corporeal frame
And even the motion of our human blood
Almost suspended, we are laid asleep
In body and becoming a living soul:
While with an eye made quiet by the power
Of harmony and the deep power of joy
We see into the life of things."

Mystics are specialists in religion, which is a matter of the heart and not the head. Sadhu Sundersingh was a mystic of a high order and his life reminds us of St. John who was one of the favourite disciples of Jesus Christ and whose gospel is considered to be the best, as it contains the esoteric teachings of the founder of Christianity, so deeply prized by lovers of true religion.

Sundersingh always said: "The head is concerned with visible things. It is the heart that sees and feels the heart of spiritual reality. My head acquiesces in what I have seen with my heart. If I had not seen them first my head would not have believed them. The heart is beyond the head."